PERSUASION
How opinions
and attitudes
are changed

PERSUASION

How opinions
and attitudes
are changed

SECOND EDITION

MARVIN KARLINS, Ph.D.

HERBERT I. ABELSON, Ph.D.

SPRINGER PUBLISHING COMPANY, INC.
New York, N. Y.

Library of Congress Catalog Card Number: 78-100098

PRINTED IN U.S.A.

To Nancy and Fay

PREFACE

The new, two-author edition of *Persuasion*, enlarged and brought up to date, retains the basic design and character of the first edition, which was written by one of us—H. A.—in 1959.

In preparing the second edition, we collaborated in selecting the studies from the literature of the sixties and in interpreting both the individual studies and the broader trends within the field. The principal author—M. K.—assembled the studies and wrote nearly all of the new text material.

Although a number of the "principles" from the first edition are retained in this work, nearly all of them include additional evidence to substantiate or modify them drawn by M. K. from more recent work. In addition, a number of studies conducted within the past five to ten years suggested additional principles, and these have been added to the book.

The second edition is larger than the first, but it remains selective. Like the first edition, it was not written as a textbook, but this edition permits the reader easier access to a broader range of current literature on opinion change than did the first.

We—the teacher of psychology and the research practitioner—have tried to accommodate the needs of three audiences: students (of psychology, sociology, journalism, and speech), the practitioners of persuasion, and the general reader who would like to be better informed about the realities of the persuasion process.

January, 1970   MARVIN KARLINS, PH.D.
Assistant Professor of Psychology,
City College of the City University of New York

HERBERT I. ABELSON, PH.D.
Executive Vice-President,
Response Analysis Corporation, Princeton, N.J.

ACKNOWLEDGMENTS

Since this book completely depends upon research conducted by social scientists and their students, our first obligation and gratitude is to the authors of the studies described here. Then, of course, there were our many colleagues who gave unselfishly of their time and skills to make our efforts more worthwhile.

Particular thanks to Gary Koeske of Pittsburgh University for his encouragement and criticism. Dr. Koeske has contributed a spirited reading of the second edition manuscript—and no critic has a sharper eye than he! The arrangement and content of the book also reflect the suggestions and criticism of LeBaron R. Foster and W. Donald Rugg of Opinion Research Corporation to the first edition, the late Thomas G. Andrews of the University of Maryland, Martin Greenberg and Richard Willis of Pittsburgh University, and our wives Nancy and Fay. We are also indebted to Professor Harry Schroder of Princeton University and to Jim Voss in his capacity as psychology department chairman at Pittsburgh.

Thanks are also due Ann Peterman of Response Analysis Corporation, Peggy Allen, Sandra Bull, and Martin Kaplan for their help in preparing the manuscript, and to the University of Pittsburgh for funds used in preparation of this second edition.

M. K.
H. I. A.

CONTENTS

1

INTRODUCTION

Take a moment to read the following statements:

> "The time has come when if you give me any normal human being and a couple of weeks . . . I can change his behavior from what it is now to whatever you want it to be, if it's physically possible. I can't make him fly by flapping his wings, but I can turn him from a Christian into a Communist and vice versa."

> "The psychologist can hardly do anything without realizing that for him the acquisition of knowledge opens up the most terrifying prospects of controlling what people do and how they think and how they behave and how they feel."

Would it surprise you to learn that a psychologist (James McConnell) wrote the first of these passages? It shouldn't. The psychologist has often viewed the control of organisms as basic to his discipline and, modesty permitting, he has often viewed his science as basic to man's destiny. Nor has he concealed his beliefs—one distinguished psychologist has even written a Utopian novel detailing how such control could be achieved in a world created and governed by psychologists (Skinner, 1948).

What might surprise you is the author of the second statement: Robert Oppenheimer, the celebrated atomic physicist. The psychologist is increasingly recognized as a person who will have much to say about the course of human events.

The psychologist's progress has not escaped public attention. On the contrary, the lay community (whose opinions are largely untempered by scientific skepticism) has credited the behavioral investigator with far more success in actually controlling behavior

1

than is the case. This attitude is clearly evident in the public's concern for "scientific mind-changers"—individuals endowed with awesome powers created in super-laboratories. That such "creatures" do not exist hardly seems to matter. John Q. Public persists in wondering about men armed with scientific know-how who can persuade anyone to do anything.

In one way, the average citizen can hardly be blamed for his unrest. His belief in the omnipotent persuader has been nurtured on a diet of exaggerations and half-truths from overzealous reporters, inflammatory pseudo-science writers, imaginative novelists, flamboyant scientists and government alarmists. What should the citizen believe? He hears vague references to subliminal advertising, sleep-learning, truth serums, sensory deprivation, and shock therapy; he reads novels like *1984, Brave New World* and *Walden Two* or, if he prefers, "non-fiction" excerpts from *The Hidden Persuaders, Battle for the Mind, The Rape of the Mind* and *The Brain Watchers;* he may see reports on the persuasive power of the mass media (did you see the Kennedy-Nixon debates?) ; or he may watch a documentary describing the brainwashing of captured prisoners of war. Perhaps as much as any event, brainwashing in North Korean prison camps has influenced Americans to feel that mind control is a reality.

Does the public have good reason to be concerned about persuasion? Has science created persuasive appeals that can control human behavior? Such questions are worth asking, even though the answers are part speculation and cannot be considered final.

Has science created persuasive appeals that *can* control human behavior? To answer this question requires, first, a passing familiarity with the history of persuasion. The *act* of persuasion is as old as man. Eve accomplished it in Eden; so did Mark Antony and so does Madison Avenue. The *incidence* of persuasion is as widespread as man—all of us have persuaded and been persuaded.

Persuasion as an *art* has been practiced for centuries. The emerging *science* of persuasion is a product of the 20th century, and is still in its infancy. The discoveries of scientific persuasion as described in this volume are probably utilized by relatively few individuals. Based on current information, then, "It is still too early to be sure" seems the most appropriate answer to the question "Has science created persuasive appeals that can control human behavior?" Even so, it is reasonable to assume that, as techniques of persuasion evolve from art to science, their effectiveness in controlling behavior will be enhanced. *How effective* remains to be seen.

How can science increase the effectiveness of a persuasive appeal?

By providing man with a systematic procedure for exploring the persuasive process. Scientific methodology provides the researcher with a means of isolating the variables he is testing—giving him a better chance of identifying the factors that are responsible for the outcome of a particular investigation.

This book is concerned with the *science* of persuasion. As such it seeks to identify, from evidence based on systematic procedure, the mechanisms involved in successful persuasive appeals. This scientific emphasis distinguishes this volume from other books on persuasion. Typically, such books reflect the experience of successful persuaders—of salesmen, newspapermen, or advisors to political candidates; they do not systematically weigh the factors responsible for the success or failure of attempts to persuade people. In *this* volume the factors and facets of persuasion are presented in order, and the evidence introduced here has been collected by scientific methods. We believe that this is the criterion that makes the book valuable.

Although scientific methodology was employed in many of the studies we report, it does not follow that the findings warrant uncritical acceptance. In a field as young as persuasion, research conclusions are open to modification and even dismissal, as additional information is amassed. Many of the results reported in this book need to be replicated and extended. Some are open to question because they were established in experiments with methodological shortcomings. Certain findings will force modification of existing "principles of persuasion" by suggesting additional factors that influence behavior change.* No one more than the researcher himself realizes the danger of interpreting data too broadly. Under slightly different conditions, an experiment might have turned out differently. The findings reported on the following pages should be viewed, then, as directives, not dogma—flexible guidelines, not rigid boundaries, in understanding behavior change. Approached in such a manner, the material in this book will, it is hoped, give the reader a fuller appreciation of the persuasive process.

---

*As research in persuasion continues it becomes increasingly evident that simple "principles of persuasion" are the exception rather than the rule. We are beginning to appreciate the complexity of the persuasive process and realize that whether or not a person is persuaded often depends on a multiplicity of interacting factors (some still not known). In moving from the undifferentiated to the more refined principles of persuasion, one is moving closer to an *effective* science of behavior control. Many investigations in the last decade have added "modifiers" to old persuasion principles. Experimenters have facilitated this process by designing investigations that could examine the interrelationships among several variables at one time.

Suggested Readings

Following each discussion a reading list (including some entries not discussed in the text) will be provided for those interested in further examination of a selected topic. Each reference was selected on the basis of: (1) relevance to the topic; (2) importance as a scholarly work; (3) availability to the reader; and (4) recency of publication.

(A) General books on persuasion:
> (1) Brown, J. A. C. *Techniques of persuasion*. Baltimore: Penguin, 1963.
> (2) Zimbardo, P. & Ebbesen, E. *Influencing attitudes and changing behavior*. Boston: Addison-Wesley, 1969.

(B) Sourcebook of experiments in persuasion:
> (3) Rosnow, R. & Robinson, E. (eds.) . *Experiments in persuasion*. New York: Academic Press, 1967. (A collection of journal articles interspersed with editorial comment.)

(C) Books discussing theories of attitude change: *
> (4) Brown, R. Models of attitude change. In *New directions in psychology, I*. New York: Holt, 1962.
> (5) Fishbein, M., (ed.) . *Readings in attitude theory and measurement*. New York: Wiley, 1967.
> (6) Insko, C. *Theories of attitude change*. New York: Appleton-Century-Crofts, 1967.
> (7) Kiesler, C., Collins, B., & Miller, N. *Attitude change: a critical analysis of theoretical approaches*. New York: Wiley, 1969.
> (8) McGuire, W. J. The nature of attitudes and attitude change. In G. Lindzey & E. Aronson (eds.) . *The handbook of social psychology* (2nd ed.), Volume III. Boston: Addison-Wesley, 1969.

---

* This book is primarily concerned with *findings* from persuasion and attitude change studies rather than with their theoretical underpinnings, and the reader interested in theory is referred to the suggested sources.

2

HOW TO PRESENT THE ISSUES

How can you best use fear to influence people?

Do you tell your audience what to think, or do you present the evidence but let them draw their own conclusions?

Can a persuasive appeal be enhanced by distracting the person listening to it?

Is a persuasive appeal more effective when it requires active or passive participation by the listener?

Are people persuaded by hearing both sides of an argument, or one side only?

When both sides of an argument are presented, which side should be told first?

When should the most important arguments be presented in a persuasive appeal?

Does information change attitudes?

Are emotional appeals more powerful than factual ones?

Is humor an effective persuasive technique?

In some circumstances a mild fear appeal (threat) is more persuasive; in other situations a strong fear appeal is better.

When the American Cancer Society representative refuses a cigarette with a polite "No thanks, I can live without it," he is attempting to change behavior by use of a fear appeal. Are such appeals persuasive? Most investigators say yes. What, then, is the relative effectiveness of mild versus strong fear appeals in changing behavior? This question has received increasing attention in the past decade due in large part to a pioneering study by Janis and Feshbach.

Specimen studies

1. Three fifteen-minute illustrated lectures were prepared on the topic of dental hygiene. All of them contained information on the causes of tooth decay, and all of them suggested proper ways of caring for the teeth and gums. The lectures differed in their descriptions of what might happen if the teeth and gums were not properly cared for. The strongly threatening lecture included the possibility of cancer among the many consequences of poor oral hygiene habits. The mildly threatening lecture condemned people who neglected their mouths to nothing worse than a few cavities. The third form of the lecture was intermediate in its degree of threat.

Three groups of students from a high school freshman class were used as subjects, one group for each form of the lecture. A fourth group of freshmen was used as controls. A week before and a week after the lecture, the students filled out a short questionnaire designed to find out about their dental hygiene practices. Immediately after the lecture, the students filled out a questionnaire which asked them how worried they were about the condition of their teeth.

Findings: The more threatening the lecture, the more the worry that was expressed immediately after it about condition of the teeth. But when the students were asked a week later how well they were actually conforming to the recommendations of the lecture, the group who had been subjected to the *least* amount of threat was found to have conformed the most.

Those who had heard the *most* threatening lecture conformed the least. In fact, there were no differences in amount of conforming between the group exposed to the most threatening form of the lecture and the control group that did not hear *any* form of the lecture. The authors concluded that under conditions where people will be exposed to competing communications dealing with the same issue, the use of a strong threat appeal will tend to be less effective than a minimal threat appeal in producing attitude change (Janis & Feshbach, 1953).

As a consequence of the Janis and Feshbach study, many individuals decided that mild fear appeals were superior to stronger ones in obtaining the desired attitude change. Such a broad generalization (based on the findings of one investigation) was certainly unwarranted. Studies conducted since the Janis and Feshbach experiment remind us that strong threats may or may not be more persuasive than mild threats; it depends on the situation under examination.*

2. 182 Yale college seniors who agreed to participate in a "student health survey" were presented with pamphlets discussing tetanus. The students were unaware that the experimenters had systematically varied the contents of each booklet in three ways:

(1) Fear level of the message: In the low-fear communication, tetanus was described as difficult to contract and relatively easy to cure. A case history, complete with black and white photographs, told of recovery from the disease following "mild medication and throat suction procedures." In the high-fear communication, tetanus was pictured as easy to contract and difficult to cure. Another case study, this one with color photographs, described death from tetanus "despite heavy medication and surgery to relieve throat congestion." In a third, no-fear message (control condition), the discussion of tetanus and accompanying case history were omitted from the pamphlets.

(2) Reported effectiveness of inoculation in preventing tetanus: In the low-effectiveness message, pamphlets contained information

---

*Some of these later studies have been critical of the Janis and Feshbach investigation. Some investigators have been unable to replicate the 1953 findings (Singer, 1965; Leventhal & Singer, 1966) and one researcher has criticized Janis and Feshbach on methodological grounds (Duke, 1967).

stating that inoculations were generally effective but did not eliminate the possibility of contracting the disease. High-effectiveness
material, on the other hand, presented inoculation as an "almost
perfect" guarantee against tetanus.

(3) Reported painfulness of the inoculation: In the high pain
message students were told that the particular shot they would receive was very painful due to the necessity of a "deep intramuscular
injection of tetanus toxoid and alum precipitate." In the no-pain
communication, discussion of discomfort was excluded from the
pamphlets.

After reading his pamphlet, each student filled out a questionnaire which asked, among other things, whether he intended to get
a tetanus inoculation. To determine if subjects actually carried out
their stated intentions, the experimenters obtained University
Health Service inoculation records for each subject.*

> *Findings:* The investigators were surprised to discover that
> there were no differences in shot-taking behavior between
> groups of students who were exposed to different information
> about how effective and how painful the inoculations would
> be. In other words, students who thought the shots would be
> painful were just as likely to get them as those who were not
> told of any discomfort; further, students who believed that the
> inoculations were not totally effective were just as likely to
> receive them as individuals who felt the shots to be a guaran-
> tee against tetanus.
>
> There was a difference, however, in student attitudes and
> behavior toward inoculations based on the fear appeal they
> had read. Students exposed to the high fear communication
> were more likely to want shots and actually get them than the
> individuals receiving the low-fear communication. The in-
> vestigators conclude: "The manipulation of fear . . . in-
> fluenced both intentions to take shots and actual shot-taking
> behavior . . . A positive relationship between fear arousal and
> persuasion was observed" (Dabbs & Leventhal, 1966).

3. In a second study demonstrating the efficacy of high fear appeals in modifying behavior, Sidney Kraus and his associates moved
from the laboratory into a community. They selected 87 indi-

---

* Information obtained from follow-up calls and letters to all subjects revealed that no students had taken shots at places other than the Health Service.

viduals from a cross section of the adult community and studied their reactions to mass media recommendations for avoiding severe eye damage while viewing a solar eclipse. The investigators' research question was straightforward: Would the average adult, confronted with a strong fear appeal ("heed these suggestions or you'll burn your eyes out") follow the recommendations included in the appeal?

> *Findings:* The authors concluded that ". . . the warnings and the recommendations of the mass media concerning the eclipse seem to have been fairly successful in affecting behavior." Even though some of the recommended procedures for watching the eclipse involved a significant outlay of effort on the part of the viewer (e.g., making "pinhole" boxes or obtaining a specific type of exposed film) a good part of the sample (41%) adopted one of the suggested procedures for viewing the eclipse. This level of compliance is relatively high for studies where fear appeals have been utilized to regulate behavior. Discussing their findings, the experimenters comment: ". . . in some cases appeals containing elements of strong fear may be used quite successfully to promote the behavior desired by the communicator" (Kraus, El-Assal & De Fleur, 1966).

Discussion

Strong or mild fear appeals: which are more effective in producing attitude change? It depends on the situation in question. Based on current evidence, strong appeals should be superior to mild ones in modifying behavior when they: (1) pose a threat to the subject's loved ones (Powell, 1965); (2) are presented by a highly credible source (Hewgill & Miller, 1965); (3) deal with topics relatively unfamiliar to the subject (Berkowitz & Cottingham, 1960; Insko, Arkoff, & Insko, 1965; Kraus, El-Assal & De Fleur, 1966); (4) aim at subjects with a high degree of self-esteem and/or low perceived vulnerability to danger (Leventhal, 1967).*

It is also possible to draw some general conclusions concerning fear appeals. It seems that fear appeals are most effective in changing behavior when: (1) immediate action can be taken on recommendations included in the appeal (Leventhal, 1967; Leventhal &

---

* The issue of strong vs mild fear appeals has received the theoretical attention of two psychologists, and the interested reader is referred to: (1) Leventhal, H. Fear: For your health. *Psychology Today*, 1967, *1*, 54–58. (2) McGuire, W. J. Attitudes and opinions. *Annual Review of Psychology*, 1966, *17*.

Niles, 1965) ; (2) specific instructions are provided for carrying out recommendations included in the appeal (Leventhal, Jones & Trembly, 1966; Leventhal, Singer & Jones, 1965) .

Suggested Readings: Fear Appeals

(1) Dabbs, J., & Leventhal, H. Effects of varying the recommendations in a fear-arousing communication. *Journal of Personality and Social Psychology,* 1966, *4*, 525-531.
(2) Janis, I., & Feshbach, S. Effects of fear-arousing communications. *Journal of Abnormal and Social Psychology,* 1953, *48*, 78-92.
(3) Kraus, S., El-Assal, E., & De Fleur, M. Fear-threat appeals in mass communication: An apparent contradiction. *Speech Monographs,* 1966, *33*, 23-29.
(4) Leventhal, H. Fear: For your health. *Psychology Today,* 1967, *1*, 54-58.

There will probably be more opinion change in the direction you want if you explicitly state your conclusions than if you let the audience draw their own.

At the end of a persuasive appeal, the speaker is often left with a problem: should he present his evidence and then stop—gambling that the audience will draw the conclusions he intended them to—or should he avoid risk and state his summary in no uncertain terms? There is experimental evidence bearing on this question.

Specimen studies

1. A tape recording of what was supposedly a radio broadcast on the topic of devaluation of currency was presented to two groups of college students. The program was identical in each case except for the ending. One group heard conclusions which were based on the statements made during the broadcast. For the other group, the program ended just before the conclusions were stated. It is worth noting that the subjects were an intelligent group, above the national average for college students. Opinion change was measured by a post-broadcast questionnaire whose purpose was disguised as a way of getting audience reaction to the program so it could be improved for later use.

> *Findings:* The group that heard the conclusions changed their opinions in the desired direction more markedly than did the group that did not hear them (Hovland & Mandell, 1952).

2. Other researchers, examining the experiment just described, were critical of it. They felt that perhaps the group that had heard the conclusions *understood* the communication better than the group that heard no conclusions. If this were so, then presenting the conclusions may have been an aid to understanding rather than a direct persuasive force. Accordingly, the following hypothesis was set up and tested: if people who do not hear conclusions actually understand the message as well as people who hear conclusions, then stating the conclusions should be no more effective in changing opinions than not stating them.

The arguments for and against United States entry into the Korean War were assembled into a clear, well-organized speech, and also into a poorly organized speech, more difficult to grasp. In both cases the arguments supported the belief that the United States followed the proper course. The subjects were new recruits to the armed forces and they were divided into four groups:

One group heard the poorly organized presentation, with the conclusion drawn that the decision to enter the war was a wise one.

A second group also heard the poorly organized presentation, but with no conclusion drawn.

A third group heard the well-organized speech with the conclusion.

A fourth group heard the well-organized speech without the conclusion.

> *Findings:* Each of the groups showed some opinion change in the desired direction. The two groups that heard the conclusions understood the arguments better. The well-organized presentations were better understood than the poorly organized presentations. Most important, if a person was intelligent enough to draw the intended conclusion for himself during the course of the speech, it made no difference in his attitude whether the conclusion was actually stated or not. Thus, stating the conclusion was more important among the less intelligent subjects. The more intelligent people tended to grasp the intended conclusion themselves (Thistlethwaite, de Haan & Kamenetsky, 1955).

3. In 1965 Weiss and Steenbock conducted a study that provides further support for the use of conclusions in persuasive appeals. They asked: Would subjects be more persuaded by a communication that contained explicit conclusions, even when those conclusions recommended actions objectionable to the listener? Two groups of college undergraduates were asked to read a communication supporting the need for a history of science course—a viewpoint strongly opposed by the students. One group read a form of the communication without a concluding section; a second group received the material given the first group *and* the concluding segment as well. A third group (control) did not read any communication. Subjects' opinions of the value of a history of science course were assessed before and after the communications were read.

> *Findings:* For initially unfavorable subjects, the communication that presented conclusions seemed more effective in changing attitudes; that is, subjects who read the communica-

tion containing the explicit conclusions (in comparison with those who did not) displayed greater receptivity toward the idea of a history of science course (Weiss & Steenbock, 1965).

Discussion

Based on the findings just outlined, why should anyone believe that conclusion-drawing by the persuader might *hurt* his cause? One argument goes this way: "If you want the audience to change their opinions, you lead them up to the desired change, but let them take the last step themselves. This is necessary, as people are more easily convinced if they think they are making up their own minds. People don't like to be told what to think." Often, however, this tactic doesn't work because of the difficulty in getting even intelligent audiences to see the implications behind the facts when these implications are left unsaid.* It is better to draw conclusions for the audience and thus increase the likelihood that they understand what you are driving at and what you want them to do (Hovland, Janis & Kelley, 1953; Fine, 1957).

This does not mean that conclusion-drawing is always the best tack to follow. In a few situations such a procedure might be ill-advised. For example, if the audience is hostile or suspicious, they may view any statement of conclusions as "propaganda." If the audience is sophisticated, they may perceive stated conclusions as an insult to their intelligence, even though, if the conclusions were left unsaid, they might think that something was being kept from them (Hovland, 1951).

Sometimes it makes little difference whether conclusions are stated or not. For example, when the issues are simple enough for everyone to know almost immediately what opinion you are trying to get them to adopt, it is not worth worrying about conclusions (Hovland, Janis & Kelley, 1953). But when the communicator is not sure of the intelligence of his audience, or the ease with which they will understand his arguments, the safe procedure is to state conclusions, and not just imply them.

This problem of implicit vs explicit argument was handled by the U.S. government in World War II (Lerner, 1951). The Office of War Information propaganda policy directive advised the propagandist to argue *implicitly* when: (1) There was a possibility that

---

* Gruner, in discussing the possible reason satire might not be an effective persuasive device, seems to agree with this observation. He says: ". . . satire, by the very nature of its distinguishing characteristic, indirectness of criticism, may lose some of its potential for changing attitudes . . ." (Gruner, 1965).

the audience might on its own stumble on the conclusion; (2) The validity of an explicit argument might be questioned; (3) You are asking the audience to take risks, and they might resent a forthright request; (4) The consequences of your argument are not known, and you do not want to take full responsibility for them.

Suggested Readings: Conclusion-Drawing

(1) Hovland, C. I., & Mandell, W. An experimental comparison of conclusion drawing by the communicator and by the audience. *Journal of Abnormal and Social Psychology*, 1952, *47*, 581-588.

(2) Weiss, W., & Steenbock, S. The influence on communication effectiveness of explicitly urging action and policy consequences. *Journal of Experimental Social Psychology*, 1965, *1*, 396-406.

Pleasant forms of distraction can often increase the effectiveness of persuasive appeals.

An old courtroom story tells of a defense lawyer who wanted to reduce the impact of the prosecution's final summation to the jury. To accomplish this, the waggish attorney placed a hat pin through the center of a cigar and began puffing it while the prosecution presented its case. The pin served as a support which prevented ashes from dropping off the end of the cigar. As the column of ash grew longer, seemingly defying gravity, the jurists focused their attention on the spectacle, oblivious to the arguments of the prosecuting attorney, who wound up losing the case. Counsel for the defense had utilized the method of *distraction* to perfection.

Specimen studies

1. Consider an experiment in 1964 by Leon Festinger and Nathan Maccoby. In this study two groups of fraternity men listened to the same anti-fraternity speech while watching movies that varied in content. In the *non-distraction condition* one group of subjects viewed a film of the speaker giving the lecture; in the *distraction condition* the second group watched a highly irrelevant silent comedy film while listening to the sound track of the first film. Festinger and Maccoby were curious: would the distracted individuals be more persuaded than the non-distracted subjects by the anti-fraternity presentation (change their opinions of fraternities in ways suggested by the speech)?

> *Findings:* Experimental results indicated that the distracted group was more persuaded by the speech—expressing more anti-fraternity attitudes than subjects in the non-distracted group who heard the same talk (Festinger & Maccoby, 1964).

Findings of the Festinger and Maccoby study cast some doubt on the attorney's strategy of distracting the jury to reduce the impact of the prosecution's argument. But then, more recent investigations cast some doubt on the Festinger and Maccoby results! For example, Haaland and Venkatesan (1968) found *less* attitude change in subjects who were subjected to visual or behavioral distraction (while listening to a persuasive communication) than in subjects hearing the same presentation without distraction. These findings, which conflict with those reported by Festinger and Maccoby, point up the fragility of scientific "facts."

With such discrepancies in experimental findings, can anything be said about the role of distraction in modifying human behavior? Yes. Recent findings point to the *type* of distraction experienced by the individual as a major factor in the persuasive process. Generally, *persuasive appeals become more powerful when presented in conjunction with moderately distracting stimuli which positively reinforce the individual.*

2. The selling-power of the "client lunch" is widely accepted in business circles. When it comes time to sign the contract—to close the deal—it is often accomplished over dessert. "A well-fed customer is a purchasing customer" was the way one salesman expressed it. In 1965, Janis, Kaye and Kirschner set out to determine empirically just how much persuasive power there really was in the bent elbow and heaping fork. The experiment they conducted was designed to determine whether the effectiveness of a persuasive appeal could be increased if it was read while eating (even when the food donor was not the source of the communication and did not endorse it).

216 Yale undergraduates were utilized as subjects in the experiment (which, for replication purposes, was run twice). In the *food condition* subjects read a series of four persuasive communications in a room well-stocked with food (soft drinks and peanuts). They were encouraged to sample the available food, which they all did. In the *no-food condition* subjects were presented with the same four communications, but in a room where no refreshments were available. In the *control condition* subjects did not receive relevant communications. All experimental subjects were asked, before and after reading the four communications, certain key questions which enabled the investigators to assess their degree of opinion change (if any) in response to the persuasive appeals.

Findings: Results of both investigations provided empirical support for sales folklore concerning the "client lunch." In the first experiment differences between the food and no-food conditions were clear-cut: subjects who ate while they read were more persuaded by each of the four communications than were those who read the same messages without food. In the second experiment the results were not quite as strong but still in support of the "food distraction-persuasibility" hypothesis. The authors conclude: ". . . in general, the extraneous gratification of eating while reading a series of persuasive communications tends to increase their effectiveness" (Janis Kaye & Kirschner, 1965).*

3. Are all distractions confronted by a subject equally effective in making him more vulnerable to a persuasive appeal? This question was examined by three investigators (Zimbardo, Ebbesen & Fraser, 1968) who subjected male college students to tape recorded persuasive appeals divergent from their previously stated points of view while they watched irrelevant visual stimuli (distractors). The first recorded speech was played while the students watched slides of scenery (a mountain, river, clouds, etc.). A second speech, similar in form but different in content, was accompanied by slides "of female nudes in rather sexually provocative poses."

Findings: Subjects were most influenced by the persuasive appeal presented in conjunction with the sexual distractors (Zimbardo, Ebbesen & Fraser, 1968).

Discussion

Food and sex—two strong positive reinforcements for the human organism. By utilizing these rewarding stimuli as distractors, psychologists discovered they could enhance the effectiveness of persuasive appeals. But what about negative reinforcers? Do they operate in a similar manner? Two investigations (Janis, Kaye & Kirschner, 1965; Zimbardo, Ebbesen & Fraser, 1968) report that negatively reinforcing distractors (foul odors and morbid medical slides) did not increase the power of a persuasive appeal. On the other hand, Simonson and Lundy (1966) found that irrelevant fear facilitated the acceptance of a written communication. It seems that evidence on this issue is somewhat contradictory, but generally points to the ineffectiveness of negatively reinforcing distractors in enhancing the power of persuasive appeals.

How distracting should a distractor be to insure maximum effectiveness in the persuasive situation? At present no hard and fast

---

* In a follow-up study James Dabbs and Irving Janis (1965) did additional work on the "eating-while-reading" variable and discovered that: "The consumption of preferred food induces a momentary mood of compliance toward the donor that is strongest at the time the food is being consumed and that decreases in strength rapidly after the food has been consumed."

rule can be stated, although an article by Rosenblatt (1966) suggests moderate distraction (as opposed to no distraction or strong distraction) might be most successful in enhancing persuasive appeals. This finding would seem to make sense: too distracting a stimulus might completely divert the subject from the message of the persuasive communication.*

In many ways the work with distraction is germane to research in general reinforcement theory (how rewards and punishments influence behavior).** Understood in the reinforcement framework, the distraction findings should not come as much of a surprise. The power of reinforcement to modify human behavior is one of the most pervasive and documented findings in modern psychology.

Suggested Readings: Distraction

(1) Festinger, L., & Maccoby, N. On resistance to persuasive communications. *Journal of Abnormal and Social Psychology,* 1964, *68,* 359-366.

(2) Haaland, G., & Venkatesan, M. Resistance of persuasive communications: An examination of the distraction hypotheses. *Journal of Personality and Social Psychology,* 1968, *9,* 167-170.

(3) Janis, I., Kaye, D., & Kirschner, P. Facilitating effects of "eating-while-reading" on responsiveness to persuasive communications. *Journal of Personality and Social Psychology,* 1965, *1,* 181-186.

---

* This point of view is adopted by McGuire, arguing from a learning theory model. See: McGuire, W. Attitudes and opinions. *Annual Review of Psychology,* 1966, *17,* 475-514.
** See, for example, Rosnow, R., & Russell, G. Spread of effect of reinforcement in persuasive communication. *Psychological Reports,* 1963, *12,* 731-735.

The impact of a persuasive appeal is enhanced by requiring active, rather than passive, participation by the listener.

If a person is asked to exert himself to gain information about a specified topic, will he be more favorably disposed toward it than if that information is "spoon fed" to him? Scientific evidence points to the "exertion of effort" (within reasonable limits) as helpful in enhancing the power of persuasive appeals.

Specimen studies

1. Let's assume that you want to persuade someone that "capital punishment should be abolished." Would you get more desired opinion change by letting him read an argument supporting your viewpoint or asking him to write an essay against the death penalty?

140 University subjects were divided into six experimental groups that either read (passive participation) or wrote (active participation) about one of three possible issues: "Puerto Rico should be admitted to the Union as the 51st state"; "courts should deal more leniently with juvenile delinquents"; and "the Secretary of State should be elected by the people, not appointed by the president."

Students who read about the issues were given persuasive communications designed to be similar in format and appeal regardless of the issue discussed. Students who wrote their own arguments about an issue were given booklets containing the title of the topic (e.g., "courts should deal more leniently with juvenile delinquents") and blank pages for composing "a strong convincing argument" in support of the topic. All subjects were given equal time, eight minutes, to read or write their persuasive appeals. A questionnaire designed to assess opinions on the three topics was administered to students just after they had read or written about the issues and again six weeks later. In the second testing session student involvement with, and recall of, the issues was also tested.

Findings: Initially, both active and passive participation led to significant opinion change. Thus, students who either read or wrote a persuasive appeal favoring a specified issue changed their opinions in the desired direction. But how long did such opinion change last? This is where the findings get interesting! In the followup testing session six weeks later, subjects who had composed persuasive appeals (active participation) displayed significantly greater persistence of the initially induced opinion change than students who had read the persuasive communication (passive participation). Further, active participation "also resulted in greater involvement (subsequent discussion of, and reading about, the topic) and superior recall of the topic and side supported." In this study, active participation was clearly superior to passive participation in long term opinion change (Watts, 1967).

Discussion

Evidence supporting "active" vs "passive" participation in enhancing the power of persuasive appeals comes from experimental findings in many different research settings. To give the reader some idea of how pervasive this principle seems to be in attitude change, here are a few sample findings from diverse experimental contexts:

(1) Role-playing, as a form of active participation, is more effective than passive participation (listening to a role-player's persuasive arguments or hearing a tape-recording of a role-playing session) in changing attitudes (Elms, 1966; Janis & Mann, 1965).

(2) Active participation, in the form of group discussion, is often more effective than passive participation (hearing lectures or reading appeals) in changing attitudes (Hereford, 1963; Lewin, 1953).

(3) Several industrial studies indicate that worker productivity and satisfaction increase when employees become actively involved with management and fellow workers in a cooperative production enterprise (the classic study in this area is Roethlisberger & Dickson, 1939).

(4) Active participation in "T-groups" or "sensitivity training" leads to marked behavior modification (Rubin, 1967).

(5) A person who actively (rather than passively) learns about a situation often changes his attitudes about that situation. Thus, visitors who took guided tours through a state school for mental defectives changed their opinions about the patients and the institution (Kimbell & Luckey, 1964); and children who studied Spanish had more positive attitudes toward Spanish-speaking peoples than children lacking such education (Riestra & Johnson, 1964).

(6) The effectiveness of a persuasive appeal is increased when exposure to the communication depends on an effortful action (Zimbardo, 1965).

(7) When individuals expect to exert more effort to hear a persuasive communication they change their opinion in the direction suggested by the communication (Wicklund, Cooper & Linder, 1967).*

Suggested Readings: Active vs Passive Participation

(1) Elms, A. Influence of fantasy ability on attitude change through role playing. *Journal of Personality and Social Psychology,* 1966, *4,* 36-43.

(2) Watts, W. Relative persistence of opinion change induced by active compared to passive participation. *Journal of Personality and Social Psychology,* 1967, *5,* 4-15.

(3) Wicklund, R., Cooper, J., & Linder, D. Effects of expected effort on attitude change prior to exposure. *Journal of Experimental Social Psychology,* 1967, *3,* 416-428.

---

* Somewhat related to this finding is a report by Sears and Freedman (1965) that persuasive communications are more effective when subjects believe they will contain novel rather than familiar arguments (even when, in fact, all the communications are identical).

When the audience is generally friendly, or when your position is the only one that will be presented, or when you want immediate, though temporary, opinion change, present one side of the argument.

When the audience initially disagrees with you, or when it is probable that the audience will hear the other side from someone else, present both sides of the argument.

The old adage "there are two sides to every story" is of particular concern to the persuader. When he is presenting his appeal, he must decide whether to discuss one or both sides of the issue. Research on one- vs two-sided appeals suggests certain guidelines for action. *

Specimen studies

1. During World War II, three groups of soldiers were asked how long they expected the war with Japan to last after Germany was defeated. Subsequently, one group was exposed to an argument showing that the war with Japan was going to be a long one. The second group received the same treatment, but in addition received some information on Japan's weaknesses. The third group was used as a control and not subjected to any communication.

> *Findings:* Results depended on how the men felt initially. Men who had earlier recorded a belief in a long war were more influenced by the one-sided presentation which supported that viewpoint. Men who thought the war would be short were influenced more by the two-sided version (Hovland, Lumsdaine & Sheffield, 1949).

2. In an experiment to see if audiences could be inoculated against counterarguments, the issue used was how long it would be before Russia had the A-bomb. The one-sided communication supported the idea that Russia would not be able to produce the A-bomb for

---

* See, also, the discussion of "inoculation" in Chapter 7.

at least five years. The two-sided treatment consisted of the same discussion but included arguments for the other side: new A-bomb factories were being built in Russia, Russia has uranium mines in Siberia, etc. Each version was presented to a different group. A third group filled out the pre-experiment questionnaire along with the other two, but heard none of the arguments. A week later, half of each group that had been exposed to a communication heard a counterargument. The counterargument included information not heard previously by either group, supporting the contention that Russia had probably already developed the A-bomb and would be producing large quantities within two years.

> *Findings:* In the group subjected to the one-sided version that Russia would need at least five more years to produce A-bombs, there was a marked opinion change in the direction of the counterargument, i.e., Russia had probably already developed the A-bomb. In the group that had previously heard arguments on both sides, there was only a slight opinion change in the direction of the counterargument. Thus the group that heard both sides was more resistant to the counterargument (Lumsdaine & Janis, 1953).

3. Another experiment was designed to reveal the influence on opinion change of communications presented in three different contexts: as a direct one-sided argument; as a two-sided debate; and as an impartial, objective presentation. The subjects were college students of both sexes; the issue was the superiority of one sex over the other. In the one-sided argument, each sex heard support for its own superiority. In the other treatments there were arguments favoring both sexes.

> *Findings:* As a result of the one-sided argument, each sex became even more biased toward its own kind than it had been at the time of the pre-experiment questionnaire. For the males, the debate also strengthened the feeling expressed before the experiment, while the impartial treatment produced attitudes of more moderation. Data for the females are not clear. In the original questionnaire, so many of them said males were superior that the responses of females could not be meaningfully tabulated (Jarrett & Sheriffs, 1953).

4. In a more recent investigation (McGinnies, 1966) some cross-cultural support was obtained for earlier "one- vs two-sided" experimental findings. Japanese university students were first asked to fill out attitude scales assessing their position toward two relevant international issues: (1) American handling of the Cuban missile crisis; and (2) visits by American submarines to Japanese ports. A week later each subject was exposed to one of four pro-American speeches, all presented in a similar manner by a Japanese dramatic arts student. The four messages were:

(1) One-sided argument—Cuban missile crisis: This presentation was based on the commentary of Ambassador Adlai Stevenson defending United States action on Cuba to the United Nations.

(2) Two-sided argument—Cuban missile crisis: In this communication "cognizance was taken of certain points raised by Premier Nikita Khrushchev on the matter of missile bases in Cuba."

(3) One-sided argument—American submarine visits: This statement was composed from Japanese editorial comments favoring such visits.

(4) Two-sided argument—American submarine visits: This speech included arguments against such visits by a "left-wing" Japanese newspaper.

After hearing one of the four speeches, each subject was given the same attitude survey he had been given a week earlier.

> *Findings:* The two-sided communication was superior to the one-sided appeal for individuals initially opposed to the position advocated. For the subjects who initially agreed with the opinions of the speaker, the one-sided communication tended to be more effective (McGinnies, 1966).

Discussion

As ordinarily defined, a frank or candid discussion includes everything known to the communicator that is pertinent to the issue. Usually, there are many sides to a question. Thus, the principle we are considering becomes more meaningful when we think not just of two sides, but of the several sides that could be presented.

---

*Findings by Rosnow (1968) introduce a note of caution in the interpretation of laboratory findings concerning the effectiveness of one- vs. two-sided communications in changing individual behavior. Based on his experimental findings, Rosnow suggests the possibility that subjects change their attitudes not on the basis of the message presented but through their perceptions of what opinion they believe the experimenter advocates. This criticism is also relevant to research reported in other sections of this book.

Why is it often effective to present more than one side of an argument? First, it implies that the communicator has objectivity. Some Voice of America research conducted in postwar Germany showed that audiences believed more of the things that they heard when programs also included admissions of shortcomings in U.S. living conditions, processes of American government and American foreign policies (Carlson & Abelson, 1956). Second, a two-sided presentation appeals to the needs of the audience to be treated as mature, informed individuals. Experimental evidence has shown that better educated men are more influenced by a two-sided treatment (Hovland, Lumsdaine & Sheffield, 1949). It is difficult to have a one-sided presentation without giving the audience an impression that they are being talked down to or spoon-fed. Such an impression will be resented by those who are genuinely informed on the topic, and those who think they are. This means almost everybody. Third, giving both sides enables the communicator to anticipate counter-arguments that the audience is rehearsing as they attend to his message. In the course of bringing up and demolishing counter-arguments, he has a chance to state the case for the other side in a less convincing way than its proponents might state it.

Here are some devices which are sometimes used to suggest candor:

(1) Adjusting the message to what is known about the audience. If there is reason to believe that the audience is unfriendly, suspicious of the communicator, or quite knowledgeable about some aspects of the issue discussed, a painstaking and conspicuous attempt at an unbiased treatment is indicated.

(2) Everybody knows that no one is perfect, and that being honest with the audience is a good way to gain their sympathy. Of course, the communicator's feeling that his position is the fundamentally right one should show through this part of the argument as well as other parts. Any number of minor shortcomings can be aired in such a way that they would appear to be negligible in the long run.

(3) If the audience already knows the weak points in your argument, it does no harm to mention them again. The authors of one experiment conclude that when facts not already known are introduced to support a counter-argument, the communicator will be weakening his position. On the other hand, if conflicting facts are extremely salient for the audience, failure to mention them may be

interpreted as a sign that the communicator has not carefully considered the other side (Thistlethwaite & Kamenetsky, 1955).

(4) Conspicuously underlying your presentation is the assumption that the audience would be on your side if they only knew the truth. The other points of view should be presented with the attitude that "it would be natural for you to have this idea if you don't know all the facts, but when you know all the facts, you will be convinced."

Suggested Readings: One- vs Two-Sided Communications

(1) Hovland, C. I., Lumsdaine, A. A., & Sheffield, F. D. *Experiments on mass communication.* Princeton: Princeton University Press, 1949.

(2) McGinnies, E. Studies in persuasion: III. Reactions of Japanese students to one-sided and two-sided communications. *Journal of Social Psychology,* 1966, *70,* 87-93.

(3) Rosnow, R. One-sided versus two-sided communication under indirect awareness of persuasive intent. *Public Opinion Quarterly,* 1968, *32,* 95-101.

When both sides of a controversial topic are presented one after the other, a number of variables determine whether the side presented first or last will be the more persuasive.

Imagine that you were required to deliver a persuasive appeal utilizing a two-sided communication. You might ask: "For the greater impact, should I present the side I favor first or last?" Researchers have asked the same question with sufficient frequency to give it a name—the *primacy-recency* issue in persuasion. The experimental question becomes: In presenting both sides of an issue, one after the other, will the message presented first (primacy) or last (recency) have the greater impact in changing behavior?

Answering the primacy-recency question has been no easy task for the behavioral investigator! Scientific opinion on the matter has passed into a third stage and is still evolving. A review of these stages should provide the reader with a keener understanding of the primacy-recency issue and further demonstrate how scientists change their minds.

Early experimental evidence pointed to a primacy effect in persuasive appeals: the message presented first seemed to be the more powerful in changing behavior. This evidence was based primarily on F. H. Lund's pioneer investigation (192), the results of which led him to postulate a "law of primacy in persuasion."

Specimen studies

1. Lund exposed three groups of subjects to the pro and con sides of issues such as protective tariff and monogamy. A counterbalanced order was used so that half the time a positive argument was first and half the time a negative argument was first. The attitudes of the subjects were measured a few days before the experimental communications, and again right after exposure.

> *Findings:* The first communication changed attitudes in the desired direction, and the second one changed them back, but not as far back as they had been before the experiment. The author concluded that the side presented first has the advantage (Lund, 1925).

Over a quarter of a century elapsed before Lund's primacy law was seriously questioned.

2. In 1952 Hovland and Mandell decided to replicate the Lund study. The conditions of his 1925 experiment were duplicated as closely as possible and fresh data collected.

> *Findings:* The results were not only different from those previously reported by Lund; they were opposite! This time there was a slight advantage for the argument presented second. Thus recency, not primacy, seemed to be more effective in the persuasive process. Because of the way the Hovland and Mandell experiment was conducted, there is reason to have somewhat more confidence in its outcome than in the findings of Lund (Hovland & Mandell, 1952).

Based on the Hovland and Mandell data (and other findings indicating a recency effect in persuasion—e.g., Cromwell, 1950), scientists began talking about a "law of recency" in place of the earlier "law of primacy." This "second stage thinking" about primacy-recency was reflected in the principle offered in the earlier edition of this book: "When opposite views are presented one after another, the one presented last will probably be more effective."

By the mid-1960's such a principle was untenable. Scientific thinking had taken yet another turn, due primarily to new findings reported by Robert Lana * and Robert Rosnow.** These investigators discovered that the primacy-recency question was more complex than initially suspected, with a large array of variables determining whether the message presented first or last will be more effective in changing behavior.***

What of primacy-recency today? Can any conclusions be drawn, any generalizations stated, concerning the order in which persuasive appeals should be presented? One of the best summary statements in the literature is offered by Rosnow and Robinson (1967): "Instead of a general 'law' of primacy, or recency, we have today an

---

* Some relevant publications include: Lana, 1961; 1963a; 1963b; 1964a; 1964b; Lana & Rosnow, 1963.

** Some relevant publications include: Corrozi & Rosnow, 1968; Rosnow, 1966; Rosnow & Goldstein, 1967; Rosnow, Holz & Levin, 1966; Rosnow & Robinson, 1967.

*** Lana and Rosnow were not alone in their efforts. The 1960's witnessed a major increase in research examining the primacy-recency question. Other studies of importance include: Insko, 1964; Miller & Campbell, 1959; Rosenbaum & Levin, 1968; Rowe, 1967; Wilson & Miller, 1968.

assortment of miscellaneous variables, some of which tend to produce primacy ('primacy bound variables'), others of which, to produce recency ('recency-bound variables'). Still others produce either order effect, depending on their utilization or temporal placement in a two-sided communication ('free variables').* Nonsalient, controversial topics, interesting subject matter, and highly familiar issues tend toward primacy. Salient topics, uninteresting subject matter, and moderately unfamiliar issues tend to yield recency. If arguments for one side are perceived more strongly than arguments for the other, then the side with the stronger arguments has the advantage—'strength' being a free variable. Another free variable is 'reinforcement.' When incidents that are perceived as rewarding or satisfying are initiated close in time to a persuasive communication, opinions tend to change in the direction of the arguments closer to the rewarding incident. When an incident is dissatisfying, or punishing, opinions tend to change in the direction of the arguments farther in time from it."

Discussion

It should be emphasized that current understanding of the primacy-recency issue does not necessarily represent final understanding of the issue. Scientific inquiry continues in this area and further insights can be expected. Until such time as the topic is satisfactorily understood it might be a good idea for the practicing persuader to utilize current information with a degree of caution.

Suggested Readings: Primacy-Recency

(1) Lana, R. E. Three theoretical interpretations of order effects in persuasive communications. *Psychological Bulletin,* 1964, *61,* 314-320.

(2) Miller, N., & Campbell, D. T. Recency and primacy in persuasion as a function of the timing of speeches and measurements. *Journal of Abnormal and Social Psychology,* 1959, *59,* 1-9.

(3) Rosnow, R. L. Whatever happened to the "Law of Primacy?" *Journal of Communication,* 1966, *16,* 10-31. (A briefer and updated version of this article appears in Rosnow, R. L., and Robinson, E. (eds.), *Experiments in Persuasion.* New York: Academic Press, 1967. See pp. 99-104.)

---

* It should be noted that some studies have tried but failed to establish primacy and recency effects (Greenberg, 1963; McGinnies, 1966; Thomas, Webb & Tweedie, 1961).

Arguments presented at the beginning or at the end of a communication will be remembered better than arguments presented in the middle.

Let us assume you were asked to serve as a subject in a psychological learning experiment. In the study you might be asked to memorize the following list of nonsense syllables:

> GAZ
> YAT
> BEK
> WAB
> FUX
> SIZ
> BOQ
> PAZ
> LUF
> KIB

When people learn nonsense syllables (or any material) and are then tested on it, almost always recollection is best for items near the beginning or the end of the list. This *serial position* effect in learning has been documented many times with many different types of stimuli. Consider, for example, the following study:

Specimen studies

1. Tannenbaum (1954) exposed twelve groups of subjects to twelve tape-recorded news broadcasts. Each broadcast consisted of twelve news items which were presented in a rotated sequence so that each group of subjects heard the items in a different order. Ten minutes after exposure the subjects were tested to see how many news items they could recall.

> *Findings:* The position of the item in the broadcast determined how well it was remembered. Recall was better at either the beginning or the end of the newscast than it was in the middle (Tannenbaum, 1954).

Persuasive appeals are normally too long to be memorized. Based on the work with nonsense syllables and the Tannenbaum findings it seems reasonable to assume that the persuader would do well to include his most important material in the opening or closing portions of his speech, where it will be learned most rapidly and remembered most readily. Further, a recent investigation by Shaw (1961) indicates that what is said first or last (versus in between) can influence actual *behavior* even if some of the communication is forgotten.

2. In real life, many decisions are made by committees and not by individuals. In such a group problem-solving situation, the recommendations of some members are ignored while the suggestions of others are adopted and become an integral part of the group decision. An individual who can consistently sway a group with his opinions is said to have *social influence* on group decisions. What variables determine a person's social influence? Many common sense answers come to mind: intelligence, extraversion, verbal fluency, dominance, etc. Shaw (1961) investigated the effects of a less obvious variable: the order in which suggestions are tendered in group interaction. His question was straightforward: would an individual's recommendation(s) be adopted by a group depending upon when it was stated during group discussion?

> *Findings:* To examine his proposed serial position effect Shaw analyzed data from two group decision-making studies. In both investigations groups of four were asked to solve problems (target locations and sequence settings for lights) through discussion and consensus of opinion. In the first study it was noted that group decisions were almost always based on the first recommendation offered—regardless of who offered it! When an analysis was performed controlling for the number of opinions given, it was found that opinions stated first or last during discussion had a significantly better chance of being adopted by the group than those offered in between. The second study, more carefully controlled than the first, reported similar findings. Thus, a serial position effect in social influence on group decisions was supported (Shaw, 1961).

Discussion

If we assume that the most important material in a persuasive appeal should be presented in the opening or closing segment of the communication, the reader might then wish to ask: "Of these two segments, which one is superior in enhancing the impact of vital information?" Conflicting experimental findings on this question (e.g., Cromwell, 1950; Sponberg, 1946) require that no final conclusion be made about whether the opening or closing parts of a communication should contain the more important material. Some speculation on this topic is possible, however. If the audience is initially not very interested in the communication, the major arguments should be presented first. Where interest is high, it seems advisable to save the "punch" for last. Here is the reasoning for this hypothesis: if you say the most important things first to an interested group, they are led to expect even more important points later on, which may make for disappointment in your audience toward the end of the message. Starting with the weak points leads the interested audience to develop expectations about what is coming that may be fulfilled by the end of the communication (Hovland, Janis & Kelley, 1953). On the other hand, a group whose motivation for your message is low is not likely to develop interest from hearing weak arguments. Therefore, in a disinterested group your chances of arousing and maintaining interest are best if the trenchant parts of the discussion are at the beginning.

Suggested Readings: Serial Position

(1) Shaw, M. E. A serial position effect in social influence on group decisions. *Journal of Social Psychology,* 1961, *54,* 83-91.

Information by itself almost never changes attitudes.

Sometimes the psychologist, utilizing scientific methods to study behavior change, discovers that a time-honored, "common sense" principle of persuasion is incorrect. Consider the belief that *information changes attitudes.* Such a viewpoint is adhered to by many individuals practicing the art of persuasion. "Give people enough of
the right kind of information," they say, "and you'll be on the way
to changing the way they feel about you." This belief is well-
expressed in the attitude of a pharmaceutical executive who
claimed: "People are suspicious of the drug industry *because they
don't know enough about it.* When the public becomes familiar
with us they won't be so distrustful."

Information changes attitudes. Is the assumption true? One
might think so. It is a seductive assumption because it seems to
make sense, is easy to communicate, not difficult to understand, and
appears to embody a solution to the problem in the statement of the
problem itself. Millions of dollars and hours have been spent de-
vising persuasive appeals based on this supposition. Most of the
efforts have been wasted.

The trouble with the assumption is that it is almost never valid.
There is a substantial body of research findings indicating that cog-
nition—knowing something new—increasing information—is effective as an attitude change agent only under very specialized conditions. One such condition is that the issue being discussed be a new
one, with no prior relationship to the individual's already-formed
attitudes. It is a rare kind of issue which meets this requirement.
New information contrary to an existing viewpoint tends to be dis-
torted to fit the existing value structure.

Specimen studies

1. One investigator, Jack Haskins, reviewed ten years of advertising
and psychological literature to see if any relationship existed between factual learning and opinion change.

> *Findings:* Based on results from 29 investigations, the author
> concludes: "Learning and recall of factual information from
> mass communications does occur. However, recall and reten-
> tion measures seem, at best, irrelevant to the ultimate effects
> desired, the changing of attitudes and behavior." Time and

time again, Professor Haskins found "no relationship between what a person learned, knew, or recalled on the one hand, and what he did or how he felt on the other." It seems clear, then, that giving a person information—"telling him the facts"—does not necessarily influence his opinions or behavior (Haskins, 1966).

Discussion

One should not come away from the above presentation believing that "implanting facts" or "providing information" is completely useless in persuasive appeals. New information can and does (1) strengthen the desired feelings which some people *already* have about a specified topic; (2) provide *existing* supporters of a topic with a way to verbalize their positive sentiments. Thus, for people who already have an opinion that the persuader wants them to have, new information can help to strengthen and solidify that opinion.

There is a striking similarity between the role of information and the role of mass media such as television and newspapers (prime sources of information) in affecting attitudes and opinions. Klapper's 1960 summary of the effects of mass media is as viable today as when it was first presented: television, newspapers and magazines strengthen viewpoints which the audience already holds. As with information, the media, by themselves, rarely if ever bring about a reversal of opinion from one point of view to its opposite.

Suggested Readings: Information

(1) Haskins, J. B. Factual recall as a measure of advertising effectiveness. *Journal of Advertising Research*, 1966, *6*, 2-8.
(2) Klapper, J. T. *The effects of mass communication*. New York: The Free Press, 1960.

Sometimes emotional appeals are more effective, sometimes factual ones; it depends on the kind of message and kind of audience.

An American writer once claimed:

> The creature man is best persuaded
> When heart, not mind, is inundated;
> Affect is what drives the will;
> Rationality keeps it still.

The question of whether emotional or factual appeals are most effective in modifying human behavior remains very much unanswered and, surprisingly, the topic of relatively few research efforts. The classic study in the area was conducted by George Hartmann over 30 years ago, yet it remains as the most creative and significant piece of research in the area to date.

Specimen studies

1. The influence of emotional vs factual appeals on voting behavior was studied in the 1936 elections. Before election time, the experimenter prepared two leaflets, both urging the recipients to vote for the Socialist Party candidates. The emotional leaflet included a description of the dire consequences of a Socialist defeat. The rational leaflet featured an outline of the Socialist Party platform. In the test city, every family in one third of the wards received the emotional leaflet, every family in another third of the wards received the rational leaflet, and the remaining families were used as controls and received neither.

> *Findings:* As it happened, Socialist candidates did better in all wards in 1936 than in previous years. However, wards where the emotional leaflet was sent out showed the greatest increase in Socialist vote over the previous election; wards where the factual leaflet was sent showed the next greatest increase, and the wards which received neither leaflet showed the least increase. The author concluded that the emotional appeal was superior (Hartmann, 1936).

2. Another study yielded some information favoring emotional appeals, as a by-product of a demonstration that laymen's attitudes toward the excess profits tax could be changed. Copies of three booklets, all written to marshal opinion against the excess profits tax, were distributed on one day with the request that they be read. An interview was conducted on the results the following day.

> *Findings:* The sober economic arguments contained in one test booklet were not as effective in influencing opinion as were the more emotional arguments in the other two booklets (Opinion Research Corporation, 1952).

3. Three forms of an article dealing with the punishment of criminals were composed and presented to three groups of university students who thought they were all reading the same written material. The forms were *identical* in their conclusion that criminals be severely punished for their crimes and *different* in the supporting evidence utilized to arrive at that conclusion. One form utilized an *emotional appeal*—aimed at inciting aggressive affect toward criminals. It vividly portrayed examples of horrid crimes and called for the reader to protect himself and his loved ones from the increasing wave of crime. A second form presented a *rational appeal* which omitted mention of actual crimes and concentrated instead on statistical data, facts, and logical arguments to support the argument for severe punishment. Readers were advised to base their opinions on "rational analysis not . . . emotion." The third form of the article, the *emotional-rational* appeal, combined sections of the first two forms and was designed to ". . . arouse and appeal initially to the same kinds of emotions and motivations as was the exclusively emotional one, and then to appeal to the intellect and critical faculties of the reader as the rational article primarily did."

Immediately after reading the article, students filled out several questionnaires, including a test designed to assess attitudes toward treatment of the criminal. Two weeks later the test was readministered to the students. At this time a fourth group of subjects (control group) who had read none of the articles also took the test.

> *Findings:* Which appeal was most successful in getting students to accept the recommendation that criminals be severely punished for their crimes? In general, it seemed that the ra-

tional arguments were more effective than the emotional appeal in changing opinions. Students reading the emotional appeal manifested a significantly *less* punitive position on criminal treatment than did the students who read the rational or emotional-rational appeal. Further, there were no differences in opinions between students reading the rational versus emotional-rational article, a finding that ". . . underscores the cogency and effectiveness of the rational arguments, since the addition of appeals to aggressive emotions did not induce a more punitive attitude."

The persuasive advantage of the rational (vs. emotional) appeal was, however, quite temporary. Two weeks later the three groups of students expressed similar opinions about treatment of the criminal—regardless of which appeal they had read! (Weiss, 1960).*

Other studies have found partial support for the superiority of factual vs emotional appeals (Bowers, 1963; Carmichael & Cronkhite, 1965; Weiss & Lieberman, 1959). In the Carmichael and Cronkhite investigation it was pointed out that the effectiveness of a particular appeal sometimes depends on the momentary mood of the audience—an important observation that is often overlooked by the persuader.

Discussion

At this time no conclusive statement is possible concerning the superiority of factual or emotional appeals.** Some studies give the nod to one type of appeal, some to the other. Part of the difficulty in drawing conclusions from the available research lies in the lack of agreement among investigators on how emotional and rational appeals are to be defined and distinguished from each other. Also, as one experimenter points out, the two kinds of appeals are not exclusive alternatives (Hovland, 1954). For example, an emotional appeal can interest a person in a problem enough to make him want to examine facts. It would seem that there is no rule about which appeal to use. Much depends on the issue to be discussed, and the composition of the audience.

---

* All groups of students who had read the articles took a more punitive stand toward criminal punishment, however, than did the individuals (control group) who had not read the communications.

** Some investigators feel that, due to the unresearchable nature of the topic, there will never be a conclusive statement about the relative superiority of factual versus emotional appeals.

Suggested Readings: Emotional vs Factual Appeals

(1) Carmichael, C., & Cronkhite, G. Frustration and language intensity. *Speech Monographs*, 1965, *32*, 107-111.

(2) Hartmann, G. A field experiment on the comparative effectiveness of "emotional" and "rational" political leaflets in determining election results. *Journal of Abnormal and Social Psychology*, 1936, *31*, 99-114.

Initial evidence indicates that humor is not an effective persuasive technique.

Research exploring the use of humor in persuasive appeals is just beginning. The primary investigator in this area, Charles Gruner, has published three studies exploring satire as a persuasive device (Gruner, 1965, 1966) and audience reactions to speakers delivering humorous speeches (Gruner, 1967).*

Specimen studies

1. Can a speech satirizing censorship be employed to change a person's attitude about censorship? This was the experimental question explored by Dr. Gruner with the aid of 254 college subjects. To answer the question Gruner first composed a satirical speech against censorship which argued ". . . since nursery rhymes are so obscene and excessively violent, they should be censored strictly." The speech was then pre-tested and rated satirical by a panel of English professors and judged as entertaining by a sample audience.

Once the speech was composed and pretested, the experiment could begin. The 254 subjects were divided into experimental and control groups and asked to fill out a "survey of student opinion on censorship." Three weeks later both groups filled out the same survey a second time—just after the experimental group had been exposed to the censorship speech (the control group did not hear the speech). One month later all subjects filled out the survey for a third and final time.

> *Findings:* Scores by both experimental and control subjects did not change significantly on any of the three censorship surveys. Thus, it is concluded that the censorship speech had no effect on subjects' attitudes. This basic finding was replicated in a later experiment by the investigator (Gruner, 1966) (Gruner, 1965).

Discussion

Gruner's findings are consistent: humor is not a potent persuasive device. Yet, because of the limited work in the area, final conclu-

---

*In his 1967 study Gruner found, among other things, that humorous speeches did not lead to greater information gain; nor were they rated more interesting than serious speeches.

sions about humor in persuasion must await the outcome of further experimentation. After all, satire is only one form of humor
and censorship is only one type of issue. Further, humor integrated
into the body of a persuasive appeal might be received differently
than humor in the form of an opening joke or witty aside. Much
research lies ahead in this area, and we would not be surprised if
a persuasion text ten years from now had some different viewpoints
on this topic.

Suggested Readings: Humor

(1) Gruner, C. R. An experimental study of satire as persuasion.
   Speech Monographs, 1965, *32*, 149-153.

3

THE INFLUENCE OF OTHERS

How well do you have to know a person before he can influence your behavior?

How important are such groups as neighbors, family, fellow workers and friends in molding opinion?

What kinds of control does the group exercise over its members' opinions?

Which members of a group are the most difficult to persuade?

Is it easier to change an opinion that has been stated publicly, or one that a person keeps to himself?

Can you increase your influence by getting people "into the act"?

A person's everyday behavior can be influenced by the actions of total strangers.

One way teenagers used to amuse themselves was to stand at a busy intersection, mouth agape in amazement, and stare intently skyward. The idea was to see how fast they could create a pedestrian bottleneck of people scanning the heavens. To this day most individuals would be hard pressed to ignore a stranger's behavior—if he piqued their curiosity.

Most people are surprised to discover just how much everyday behavior is vulnerable to manipulation by strangers. Such surprise is not surprising! What makes manipulation by strangers particularly insidious is that the controlled individual is often unaware his actions are being influenced. Consider, for example, the following studies: Would you have acted differently from the unsuspecting subjects? *

Specimen studies

1. Imagine yourself driving along. To your right you spot a disabled auto (flat left-rear tire) resting on the shoulder of the roadway. Next to the vehicle, in full view of passing traffic, is a young lady obviously needing assistance. A fully inflated tire is propped up against the car's fender. Would you stop to help? If the answer is "no," might you have replied "yes" if, before you saw the woman in distress, you had just passed another car with a flat—this time with a lady watching a man changing a tire? In other words: would you be more likely to offer help once you had observed someone else engaged in a similar act of assistance? To answer this question James Bryan and Mary Ann Test (1967) "staked out" a section of highway and conducted an investigation. There were two experimental conditions in the study. In the first condition two disabled cars were spaced a quarter mile apart on a highway (the test was constructed so a driver going by one vehicle had to pass the second as well). Each automobile had a flat tire and a female standing nearby. The lady near the first vehicle (the "model car") was being aided by a man who was changing the tire; the woman standing by the car down the road (the "control car") was alone. In the

---

*Research work in "social facilitation"—where an individual performs differently in a group than when alone—is relevant here. See, for instance, Zajonc, R. B. Social facilitation. *Science,* 1965, *149,* 269–274.

second condition the model car was removed so that only the control car and the unassisted girl remained.

The experiment was run in four phases, twice for the model condition (both cars present); twice for the no-model condition (control car only). Each phase of the investigation was terminated after 1,000 cars had transversed the designated section of highway. The dependent variable was the number of people who stopped to offer aid to the young lady standing near the control car.

> *Findings:* Approximately 2.5% of the passing automobiles (93 of 4000 cars) stopped next to the stranded motorist. When the model and control car were both on the highway, 58 individuals offered aid; when the control car was presented alone, only 35 such offers were forthcoming. This numerical difference is statistically significant and supported the hypothesis that "helping behaviors can be significantly increased through the observation of others' helpfulness." Stated another way: the actions of a perfect stranger changing a car tire influenced the behavior of other individuals toward performance of the same task (Bryan & Test, 1967).*

2. In a now classic experiment, the subject's task in each of several trials was to match a line a few inches long against three other lines of differing length. The subject then said which of the three comparison lines was equal in length to the test line. Each real subject found himself in a group with seven other subjects who were confederates of the experimenter and knew in advance what they were going to say. At each trial the real subjects were called upon last for their judgments; the accomplices meanwhile had made many wild deviations from fact. The critical question was: in a situation as apparently obvious and as easy as guessing the length of lines (there were absolutely no tricks) could a group of strangers exert any influence on the individual?

> *Findings:* It certainly could! The errors made by the confederates were quite large. Yet one-third of the real subjects gave in to the false majority judgments in at least half of the trials. To make sure that the task of line-judging was not in reality a difficult one, the same problems were given to a con-

---

* In two further studies reported in the same article the authors found that frequency of money donations (placed in a Salvation Army kettle) could be increased by letting prospective donors observe a "stooge" contributing to the fund.

trol group whose members judged the lines when alone. They made virtually no errors. The experimenter pointed out: "The critical subject—whom we had placed in the position of a *minority of one* in the midst of a *unanimous majority*— faced, possibly for the first time in his life, a situation in which a group unanimously contradicted the evidence of his senses." The judgments of strangers carried more weight with the subjects than their own eyes did! (Asch, 1956).*

3. Another classic study was conducted by Muzafer Sherif utilizing the "autokinetic effect." A person is seated in a perfectly dark room, then a stationary pinpoint of light is turned on, and after a few moments the subject reports that the light is moving. He does so, even though the light is stationary, because the absence of any other visible object deprives him of the usual points of reference which are commonly in his visual field, such as walls and floor and furniture. Different people will see the light moving in different directions and at varying distances from its starting point. Every subject in this experiment was first tested alone. For each of several trials, he was asked to report how many inches the light moved each time it was turned on. After the subject had settled down to giving roughly the same answer at each trial, he was excused from the room and another subject was brought in and tested. After all the subjects had been tested individually, they were brought together in groups of twos and threes and put through the experiment again so that each of them could hear the reports of the others.

Findings: Even though each group member started out with the estimate he had developed individually, after a few trials all the members of a group were making roughly the same judgment. They had developed a group norm. To put it another way, the group had provided an orientation for them that did not exist before. To make sure this was the case, the experiment was run in reverse: first the group sessions, then the individual ones. In line with expectations, the norm that was developed in the group sessions was maintained in the private ones (Sherif, 1952).

---

* The initial study reported by Asch has been replicated and extended by numerous investigators. Current findings indicate that the conformity effects found by Asch are not as simple as initially believed. See, for example, Becker, Lerner & Carroll, 1966; Gerard, Wilhelmy & Connolley, 1968; Schulman, 1967; and Stricker, Messick & Jackson, 1967.

4. A busy downtown intersection in a large city provided the setting for another demonstration of social influence by strangers. Vehicular traffic is controlled at this intersection by the conventional red, amber, and green signal lights. Pedestrian traffic is also controlled by signals: signs flash from "walk" to "wait" at the appropriate times. By arrangement with the city police department, no policemen were on duty at the intersection during the times that the experiment was being conducted.

The main issue for investigation was whether pedestrians would violate the "wait" signal more often if they saw someone else violating it than if there were no violator. Another objective of the study was to determine whether the social class that the violator apparently represented (by the way he was dressed) had any effect on other people's behavior.

The data were collected on three successive days, for three different one-hour periods. The experimenters made use of a confederate who dressed in two different ways: (1) When he played the part of a high status person he wore a freshly pressed suit, shined shoes, white shirt, tie and straw hat; (2) his low status outfit consisted of well-worn scuffed shoes, soiled and patched trousers, and an unpressed blue denim shirt. The confederate conformed to and violated the "wait" signal an equal number of times in his high status and in his low status clothes. In addition, pedestrians were observed under a control condition when the confederate was not on the scene at all. Observations were made on 2103 pedestrians who crossed the street during the hours of the experiment. Children and physically handicapped people were not included in the tallies.

Findings: Nearly all (99%) of the pedestrians obeyed the "wait" sign under normal conditions, that is, when no confederate was present. The same percentage obeyed under one of the experimental conditions: when the confederate was present and obeying the signal himself. This was true whether he was in his high or low status clothes. When the confederate violated the signal, however, he was instrumental in inducing others to violate it. When he disobeyed the signal in his low status clothes, 4% of the other pedestrians disobeyed. When he violated the signal in his high status clothes, 14% of the other pedestrians also violated it. The findings led to two conclusions: (1) a violator influences others to disregard the prohibition; (2) a violator who seems to be of high status can influence more people than a violator of apparently low status (Lefkowitz, Blake & Mouton, 1955).

5. Another experiment also tested the influence of a confederate in a setting where subjects could choose to conform to or violate a prohibition. The data for this experiment were collected near the main door of a university classroom building. The locale had these advantages for research purposes: (1) the pathway leading from the main sidewalk to the main entrance of the building was used only by people who wanted to enter the building; (2) the building had a side entrance which was much less convenient to reach.

From a pretest on 250 students of ten different signs, three signs of graded strength (as determined by the pretest) were chosen for this experiment. The strong sign was "Positively No Admittance—Use Side Entrance." The sign of intermediate strength was "Please Use Other Entrance." The weak sign was "Absolutely No Admittance." The major difference in these signs is that the strong one prohibits entry but supplies an alternate way of getting into the building. The second one is specific about the alternative but forbids entry only by implication. The weak sign forbids entry but supplies no alternative.

During the course of the experiment each of the three signs was posted in turn on the main door of the building. The test subjects were the 90 people who happened to be on their way to enter the building during the hours of the experiment. In addition to the variable of sign strength, the influence of others on entrance behavior was varied in three ways. In two of the variations, an experimenter's confederate approached the main door about ten paces ahead of a subject, and read the sign. In one case, the confederate then turned and went around to the side door. In the other case, the confederate entered the building by the main door (disregarding the sign). In the third variation there was neither a confederate nor any other person for the subject to observe.

> *Findings:* A definite difference in the behavior of the subjects was produced by each of the signs. As might be expected, the strong sign was the most effective prohibition, the weak sign least effective. The behavior of the subjects was also affected by the actions of the experimenter's confederate. When no one else was walking toward the entrance, the subjects violated the sign more than when the confederate was present and conforming. The most violations were observed among the subjects when the confederate was present and violating the sign (Freed, Chandler, Mouton & Blake, 1955).

6. An additional demonstration of how strangers can influence a person's behavior is found in an experimental situation where 90 students with different degrees of thirst were faced with a sign over a drinking fountain which read, "Do not use this fountain." The students had been led to believe that the experiment they were to take part in was a study of taste preferences rather than what it actually was: a study of social influence. Different degrees of thirst were induced by asking the students to eat varying numbers of crackers, some treated with hot sauce or belladonna. After eating the crackers, the subjects were asked to step into the hall for a few moments on the pretext that the next part of the "taste experiment" was not ready to begin.

While in the hall, the students saw the water fountain and the sign prohibiting its use. While in this location, some of the subjects observed a person violating the prohibition. Other subjects saw a person conforming to the prohibition. Still another group of subjects, a control group, were not exposed to anyone else's reactions to the sign.

> *Findings:* The data confirm the results of the other experiments: subjects who saw someone else violate the prohibition were more likely to drink from the fountain themselves than were the subjects who observed conforming behavior (Kimbrell & Blake, 1958).

Discussion

It seems that an individual's simple everyday behavior (like obeying signs) can be modified by total strangers. But is this not a moot point? "So what?" you say, "If this is behavior control it is too innocuous to consider." This is partially true: the persuasive power of a stranger is diminished on issues of *central concern* to an individual. Yet, one would do well not to underestimate the manipulative power of strangers, particularly when many of them exert pressure on the individual at once (e.g., in crowds).* Man changes his behavior frequently in adjusting to the actions of other human beings, whether he knows them or not.**

---

* George Orwell gives a graphic example of just such multiple influence in his essay "Shooting an elephant," from the book *Shooting an Elephant,* Harcourt, Brace & World, Inc., 1950. (See p. 154–163.)

** The power of a stranger to influence behavior is highly striking when others perceive him as an authority figure. See, for example, Milgram's "obedience studies" (Milgram, 1963, 1964).

Suggested Readings: Influence of Strangers on Behavior

(1) Bryan, J., & Test, M. Models and helping: Naturalistic studies in aiding behavior. *Journal of Personality and Social Psychology*, 1967, *6*, 400-407.

(2) Lefkowitz, M., Blake, R., & Mouton, J. Status factors in pedestrian violation of traffic signals. *Journal of Abnormal and Social Psychology*, 1955, *51*, 704-706.

A person's opinions and attitudes are strongly influenced by the groups to which he belongs and wants to belong.

Group control over individual behavior is a well-documented phenomenon in psychological research. Most people are cognizant of this information and utilize it (sometimes a bit too vigorously) in dealing with others. Take the case of a Princeton University undergraduate who was asked why he wouldn't accept a blind date with a Sarah Lawrence coed. "Wrong type," was his reply. "Long hair . . . too liberal . . . I want something a bit more refined from, say, Manhattanville." Implicit in this student's reply was acceptance of the principle: "A person's opinions and attitudes are strongly influenced by the groups to which he belongs and wants to belong." This particular undergraduate assumed the existence of a Sarah Lawrence group with norms that were adhered to by the college coeds and reflected in their behavior. As far as he was concerned, one Sarah Lawrence girl was the same as the next: carbon copies—products from the same mold.

Our Princeton undergraduate is not alone in making judgments about individuals based on their group affiliations. It is well-known that American culture is saturated with images and caricatures of various groups. These "pictures in our heads" which Walter Lippman first identified as stereotypes have come to be regarded as highly significant factors in intergroup and interpersonal relations. Most of us, at one time or another, have predicted a person's behavior by knowing his group membership. Further, such judgments are not limited to a few groups; they seem to encompass groups of all sizes and complexity, from a neighborhood clique to national and ethnic groups (Karlins, Coffman & Walters, 1969).

Now, of course, no group existing today has so much influence on the individual as to obviate personality differences between members. Group members are not mirror images of each other. Thus, it is quite likely that our Princeton student, if he were objective, would find many girls at both Sarah Lawrence and Manhattanville with similar characteristics. Yet, there is no doubt that group norms do regulate significant human behavior to a large degree; and the person who tries to understand individual actions within a group framework is using a sound guideline for his inquiry.

Some of the best and most important work on group influence was conducted by social scientists in the 1950's. The power of groups in regulating members' behavior was documented in many different settings, including military academies (Dornbusch, 1955), industrial shops (Roy, 1952) and doctors' offices (Coleman, Katz & Menzel, 1957). Findings from studies in the past decade continue to illuminate the pervasive control by groups, even over things as basic as a person's own perceptions!

Specimen studies

1. In an investigation by Koslin, Haarlow, Karlins and Pargament (1968), it was demonstrated that something as "personal" as visual perception is vulnerable to distortion through group influence. The setting for this experiment was an athletics-oriented boys' camp in Southern Canada. The subjects were 29 adolescent boys billeted in four different cabins.

In the first part of the study the group status of each camper was determined. This was done by observing each cabin group extensively to find out which individuals were leaders and which were followers. Once the status structure of the group was known, the second part of the experiment was undertaken. Here, each camper was asked to judge the performance of his cabinmates on several tasks of central concern to the group, including two related to athletics—rifle and canoe tasks.

The hypothesis of the study predicted a correspondence between group status and the extent to which the performances of group members would be over- or under-estimated when every group member made such judgments of every other member on the rifle and canoe tasks. In other words, it was suspected that regardless of how the campers actually performed on the tasks, individuals with low status would be judged as inferior shooters and canoers, while individuals with higher status would be judged as superior in these skills.

> *Findings:* As predicted, there was a definite relationship between a camper's status position in the group and other members' perceptions of his performance on tasks (rifle and canoe) of central concern to the group. Thus, a correspondence between group status and members' cognitions was found (Koslin, Haarlow, Karlins & Pargament, 1968).[*]

---

[*] For another example of group membership influencing individual perception see: Hastorf, A., & Cantril, H. They saw a game: A case study. *Journal of Abnormal and Social Psychology*, 1954, *49*, 129–134.

2. Even a person's capacity to endure pain seems open to group influence. In a study by Lambert, Libman, and Poser (1960), Jewish and Protestant women college students were individually tested with a "doctored" sphygmomanometer (used for measuring blood pressure). This particular model had sharp rubber projections sewn into its inner surface which gouged the subject's arm when air pressure was increased. In the first phase of the investigation, each coed's pain endurance limit was assessed by increasing pressure in the sphygmomanometer until she pronounced the pain intolerable. Once the subject's pain tolerance level was known, she was told that a retest (for reliability purposes) would be necessary in about five minutes. At this point the experimenter casually informed the Jewish subjects about research reporting that Jews as a group can take less pain than Christians. Protestant subjects were given the same story in reverse: Christians can take less pain than Jews. Two control groups (one Jewish and one Protestant) received no information between their two tests. How much pain did the various groups of subjects endure in the second testing session?

> *Findings:* The intolerable pain limits of both the Jewish and Protestant subjects were significantly increased. In other words, both sets of subjects were willing to endure more pain the second time before they "hollered uncle." No such differences were found for control subjects. The authors conclude: "Subjects do change their patterns of behavior in meaningful ways when they alternately refer themselves to different membership groups, in this case first as university students contributing to a scientific investigation and then as members of a particular religious group" (Lambert, Libman & Poser, 1960).

3. An excellent investigation of adolescent drinking patterns in natural cliques was conducted by C. Norman Alexander in 1964. This investigator studied the relationship between a teenager's group affiliation and his alcohol consumption.

> *Findings:* A teenager's group affiliation did influence his alcohol consumption. From his data Alexander concluded that: (1) in groups where individuals are mutually attractive to one another there is a tendency for members to exhibit the same drinking habits; and (2) where there is agreement

among group members about the acceptability of an activity such as alcohol consumption, group standards tend to develop which support the activity (Alexander, 1964).

Suggested Readings: Group Influence

(1) Alexander, C. Consensus and mutual attraction in natural cliques: A study of adolescent drinkers. *American Journal of Sociology,* 1964, *69,* 395-403.

(2) Koslin, B., Haarlow, R., Karlins, M., & Pargament, R. Predicting group status from members' cognitions. *Sociometry,* 1968, *31,* 64-75.

(3) Lambert, W., Libman, E., & Poser, E. The effect of increased salience of a membership group on pain tolerance. *Journal of Personality,* 1960, *28,* 350-357.

The person is rewarded for conforming to the standards of the group and punished for deviating from them.

The concept of "honor among thieves" seems alien to many people. Why should a captured criminal refuse to inform on his buddies, even in cases where their negligence led to his arrest? Understood in a group context, such behavior is eminently reasonable. We have claimed that a person is rewarded for conforming to the standards of the group and punished for deviating from them. But to what group does the criminal belong? Certainly his allegiance is not to "establishment" groups. To the lawbreaker the mores of the criminal group become his mores; he behaves in accordance with the reward and punishment sanctions imposed by this group. And one of the most sacrosanct dictates of the criminal code is never to "squeal to the cops." The "stoolie"—the man who "rats" on other criminals—is punished by his peers. The man who keeps his mouth shut is rewarded for his behavior. Is it any wonder the criminal refuses to cooperate with authorities? Such behavior is respected in the criminal culture, the culture of prime importance to the lawbreaker.

All groups attempt to regulate members' behavior by application of rewards and punishments. Sometimes the "systems of reinforcement" are highly structured, formal, and clearly understood, as in the case of the military. Other times they are more flexible, informal, and open to interpretation, as in the academic profession. Some examples of how groups utilize rewards and punishments to control members' actions are presented in Specimen Studies 1 and 2 below.

Specimen studies

1. Work groups in industrial plants are notorious for their application of rewards and punishments to keep members in line. These sanctions are so powerful they often take precedence over the reward and punishment system imposed by management in the same plant. Consider, for example, a classic series of studies at the Hawthorne division of Western Electric Company around 1930. One such investigation focused on a "bank wiring room" where a group of 14 workers (nine wiremen, three soldermen and two inspectors) assembled terminal banks for use in telephone exchanges.

These men were paid on the "incentive system"—the more they produced, the more they were paid. The assumption behind the wage system was simple enough: every employee would work harder to amass a higher salary. The system failed. Why? Because the informal social organization of the workers in the bank wiring room had established a more powerful set of rewards and punishments (than money) to keep output at a fixed level.

In discussing the Western Electric investigations, George C. Homans gives an excellent description of how work-group sanctions operate to control the behavior of individual laborers: "The working group had also developed methods of enforcing respect for its attitudes. The experts who devised the wage incentive scheme assumed that the group would bring pressure to bear upon the slower workers to make them work faster and so increase the earnings of the group. In point of fact, something like the opposite occurred. The employees brought pressure to bear not upon the slower workers but upon the faster ones, the very ones who contributed most of the earnings of the group. The pressure was brought to bear in various ways. One of them was 'binging.' If one of the employees did something which was not considered quite proper, one of his fellow workers had the right to 'bing' him. Binging consisted of hitting him a stiff blow on the upper arm. The person who was struck usually took the blow without protest and did not strike back. Obviously the virtue of binging as punishment did not lie in the physical hurt given to the worker but in the mental hurt that came from knowing that the group disapproved of what he had done. Other practices which naturally served the same end were sarcasm and the use of invectives. If a person turned out too much work, he was called names, such as 'Speed King' or 'The Slave'" (Homans, 1951).*

2. A study by Calvin (1962) provides us with insight into the dynamics of reinforcement in regulating group behavior. As an educational demonstration, the 24 members of an introductory psychology class at Hollins College experienced the power of rewards and punishments first hand: by reinforcing specified behaviors of their 500 schoolmates and observing the results. The experimental question was: could simple verbal reinforcement serve to regulate choice of wearing apparel among college coeds? To answer the question, the 24 "experimenters" decided to compliment all girls

---

* For another example of how work group sanctions can regulate production see: Roy, D. Quota restriction and goldbricking in a machine shop. *American Journal of Sociology*, 1952, *57*, 427–442.

who wore blue clothes on specified days. Later, reinforcement was switched to girls dressed in red clothes. Would such verbal accolades lead to an increased wearing of the reinforced colors?

> *Findings:* Yes. Before the wearing of blue clothes was reinforced, one-fourth of the school's coeds dressed in blue outfits. After reinforcement the figure rose to 38%. Reinforcing red clothes led to a similar outcome: wearing the color red doubled after reinforcement (11% before reinforcement, 22% after). All these findings are statistically significant and point up the pervasive influence of reinforcement in controlling human behavior (Calvin, 1962).

Discussion

Group sanctions do not stop at the workplace—they often "follow us home" and dictate the ways we behave in our neighborhoods.* This is particularly true in suburbia, where crowded living conditions among neighbors of similar background and occupational circumstances give rise to norms regulating standards of residential life. In some communities of executives of the same corporation, certain purchases (for example, a grand piano) are reportedly not made when the family can afford them, but only when the executive's standing in the company shows he "is ready for it" (Whyte, 1952). One survey of consumer habits that investigated informal communication networks, or neighborhood groupings, showed remarkable similarity among the major appliances common to each household in the "net" and differences between households in the groupings and other households, even within the same block. In speaking about the acceptability of a given kind of appliance in the neighborhood (e.g., is it okay to buy a dishwasher) the author says, "It is the group that determines when a luxury becomes a necessity." The study showed strong criticism of the family without a TV set in a neighborhood where almost everybody had one. The few without were said to be depriving their children of the educational benefits of the medium. In this context, the author points out: "People must rationalize their purchases, and soon the nonpossession of the item becomes an almost unsocial act, an unspoken aspersion on the others' judgment or taste" (Whyte, 1954).**

---

* A classic study in this area was conducted by Festinger, Schachter and Back in 1950. (See: Festinger, L., et al., *Social pressures in informal groups: a study of human factors in housing.* New York: Harper, 1950).
** To fully appreciate the extent of "neighborhood control" in patterns of consumer purchasing see: Whyte, W. H. The outgoing life. *Fortune,* July, 1953.

Suggested Readings: Group Sanctions

(1) Calvin, A. Social reinforcement. *Journal of Social Psychology,*
     1962, *56*, 15-19.

People who are most attached to a group are probably least influenced by communications which conflict with group norms.

Specimen studies

1. Lucille Nahemow and Ruth Bennett (1967) studied the impact of group influence on 96 residents of a home for the aged. A 20-item "conformity scale" was constructed, each question designed to assess the subject's willingness to act in accordance with the norms shared by residents of the home. For example, if a subject replied "yes" to the following questions he would be conforming to group norms: (1) "Do you always ask permission and show your pass when you leave the Home?" (2) "Do you always make your visitors leave when visiting hours are over?" (3) "Would you keep yourself from talking to one staff member about another staff member whom you didn't like even if you had a good reason?" The higher the score a person achieved, the more he conformed to group norms. A score of "0" indicated total nonconformity; "20," total conformity.*

Subjects were also exposed to two persuasive appeals that were *in opposition* to the norms of the resident group. One appeal argued that tipping the home's employees should be abolished; the other that room-sharing should be practiced. The subjects' opinions on the two proposals were assessed before and after the persuasive communications. The question under investigation: Will subjects most committed to the norms of the resident group (as measured by scores on the 20-item conformity scale) be more resistant than less committed residents to persuasive communications against group norms (assessed by responses to the persuasive appeals) ?

> *Findings:* The residents who conformed most closely to group norms were *least* likely to be persuaded by appeals arguing against group norms (Nahemow & Bennett, 1967) .

2. Twelve boy scout troops filled out questionnaires that asked about a number of things: how much they valued their member-

---

* "Conforming individuals evaluated the home highly and tended to regard it as a positive reference group while simultaneously indicating a lack of interest in people and events outside the home."

ship in the scouts, what they thought of the various kinds of wood-craft activities (typical of the scouting program), and what they thought of several of the activities characteristic of city life (visiting museums, participating in civic affairs, and a number of appealing things to do in town). The woodcraft/city life questions were an indirect way of getting at what scouts do as opposed to what non-scouts of the same age groups do. A week later an adult whom the scouts did not know went to the troop meeting and in a talk to the boys suggested that they would be better off learning about and participating in the many things the city offered them than wasting their time on woodcraft activities. Immediately after his talk the woodcraft/city life scale was readministered.

> *Findings:* The scouts who valued their membership highly were little swayed by the talk; those who cared less about belonging were influenced much more (Kelley & Volkart, 1952).

3. In another experiment, Catholic college students anonymously answered a questionnaire tapping their opinions and practices on matters related to Catholic beliefs and norms. While they were working on their answers, some of them were shown the alleged responses of other students to these same questions. The responses they were shown would not generally be the most acceptable kind for Catholics. How frequently the students said they went to church was the basis for inferring how much value they placed on being Catholic. Responses were tabulated separately for those who valued their membership in the Catholic church highly and those who valued it little.

> *Findings:* The communication had a much greater influence on those who placed little value on their membership than for those for whom church membership was important (Kelley, 1955).

Suggested Readings: Group Involvement

(1) Nahemow, L., & Bennett, R. Conformity, persuasibility and counternormative persuasion. *Sociometry,* 1967, *30,* 14-25.

Opinions which people make known to others are harder to change than opinions which people hold privately.

Specimen studies

1. Earlier in this chapter Asch's "length of line" experiment was described (Specimen Study 2, p. 43). One finding of this study revealed that individuals who did not yield to majority influence in the first few line-judging trials tended to remain independent through the remainder of the experiment. One psychologist, Harold Gerard, puzzled over the finding. Why, he asked, would a subject remain unyielding to majority opinion trial after trial? At the outset of the experiment such opposition to group consensus might be understandable, but in the face of continuing opposition this type of adamant behavior is rather unusual. Gerard hypothesized that the subject's steadfast unwillingness to bow to consistent majority opposition was a function of his public commitment to his judgment. Professor Gerard reasoned: "In a face-to-face situation an avowal of a discrepant stand is a public commitment to the group of one's stalwartness. Any change in this behavior in the direction of yielding would violate this image not only to oneself but to the group. We would therefore expect that an individual who started out deviating publicly in Asch's experiment would, as Asch discovered, continue to do so in the face of continued disagreement. If, however, we assume that the individual's confidence decreases with successive disagreement, we would expect that where the individual *has not* been identified publicly with a deviant stand he would tend, with successive disagreement, to yield his own judgments and adopt those of the others."

To test his hypothesis Gerard re-ran the Asch study with a crucial modification: in one experimental condition the subjects made their line-judging estimates anonymously (in separate cubicles). In a second condition subjects made their responses in face-to-face confrontations, as in the original Asch experiment.

Findings: The results supported the hypothesis. For subjects who initially disagreed with the majority opinion, those in the *public* (face-to-face) condition maintained their views on later trials more frequently then persons in the *private* (anonymous) condition. It seems that people are more committed to behavior they undertake in a public situation (Gerard, 1964).

2. In another experiment, speeches were prepared that argued each side of this issue: that it would be desirable to lower the minimum voting age. About 100 high school students heard first one speech, then the other. In the interval between the two opposing speeches, all of the students were asked to write a short essay stating their own opinions. Half of the students were told that their essays might be published under their names in the school paper. This was the "commitment" group. The other students wrote their essays without the expectation that their opinions would be made public. This was the control group. Half of the students in each of these groups heard the affirmative speech first, and half heard the negative speech first.

> *Findings:* It seems fairly definite that ". . . the commitment procedure increased the subjects' resistance to influence by communication." Relatively few of the students who expected their opinions to be published changed as a result of subsequent communication. In comparison, relatively many of the students changed their opinions who did *not* write for 'publication' " (Hobart & Hovland, 1954) .*

Discussion

Why should people be influenced at all by the judgments of others? For one thing, each day we rely on the judgments of other people as guides to our own behavior. A man's wife looks out of the window and predicts rain, so he takes a raincoat to the office. A fellow commuter doesn't like the way our car engine sounds, and we take his advice to consult a mechanic. The more novel and/or ambiguous a situation the more likely we are to value and follow the opinions of others.

Much has been said lately about our trend toward conformity. Children are taught that a paramount virtue is getting along with other people. The stress is more on the need for agreement than

---

* Public commitment can also make an individual's attitudes more immune to counter-propaganda. See: Hovland, C., Campbell, E., & Brock, T. The effects of "commitment" on opinion change following communication. In C. I. Hovland et al., *The order of presentation in persuasion.* New Haven: Yale Univ. Press, 1957.

on the principles which may have to be sacrificed in order to reach agreement. Social influences are seen as inducing compromise and harmony as ends in themselves rather than as ways of reaching more substantial goals.

Why should a publicly expressed opinion be more resistant to influence than an opinion that is privately held? One hypothesis is that social influence works two ways: it induces people to conform to their *own* judgments as well as to the judgments of others. Whenever a person commits himself to an opinion the influence is in the direction of conforming to his own judgment.

So far the studies described here have shown that a publicly expressed opinion is more resistant to change than an opinion which is privately held. There is another aspect to this situation. Opinions sometimes undergo change in the very process of being made public. One study has shown that when people think there is a difference between their opinions and the opinions of a group they are with, they will tend to change their opinions in the direction of group consensus if they are asked to express a point of view (Raven, 1959). Other experimenters emphasize the importance of the conflict that results when a person is asked to express an opinion which is contrary to what he believes (Hartley & Hartley, 1952). In some elaborately contrived experiments it has been shown that the greater the conflict between what a man thinks and what he says, the more likely will his opinions tend to change in the direction of what he says (Festinger & Carlsmith, 1959).

In considering the implications of the commitment experiments, two researchers suggest that social influences can be used to strengthen individual integrity, and not just to undermine it. "Groups can demand of their members that they have self-respect, that they value their own experience, that they be capable of acting without slavish regard for popularity. Unless groups encourage their members to express their own, independent judgments, group consensus is likely to be an empty achievement" (Deutsch & Gerard, 1955).

Suggested Readings: Public vs Private Commitment

(1) Gerard, H. B. Conformity and commitment to the group. *Journal of Abnormal and Social Psychology*, 1964, *68*, 209-211.

Audience participation (group discussion and decision making) helps to overcome resistance.

In Chapter 2 it was claimed that "the impact of a persuasive appeal is enhanced by requiring active rather than passive participation by the listener." Evidence presented in this section increases our confidence in the validity of such a claim.

The "classic" study in this area was conducted by the eminent social psychologist Kurt Lewin during World War II and is presented as Specimen Study 1 below. Since that time other investigations have been performed which document the value of audience participation in changing behavior (e.g., Bitter, 1963; Hereford, 1963).

Specimen studies

1. During World War II, the task of a group of social scientists was to find ways to persuade housewives to serve unpopular meats (beef hearts, sweetbreads and kidneys) to their families. One experiment made use of six groups of Red Cross home nursing volunteers. Three of these groups heard a lecture linking use of these foods with the war effort, showing their nutritional value, and indicating how deliciously they could be prepared. Mimeographed recipes were distributed. The other three groups heard only a brief introduction. Then the experimenter took a poll to see how many of the women had served these organ meats before. Instead of hearing a lecture, they were drawn into a discussion of why housewives had trouble preparing, serving and gaining acceptance for organ meats. At the end of the meeting, the women were asked to raise their hands if they planned to serve an organ meat during the next week.

> *Findings:* A follow-up showed that 3% of the women who heard the lectures served one of the meats never served before, compared with 32% of the women who had participated in the group discussion sessions (Lewin, 1953).*

2. This study, also from World War II, had to do with persuading management to change a part of its personnel policy. During the

---

* Although the majority of investigations substantiate the effectiveness of group discussion in changing attitudes, some studies disagree (Bennett, 1955; Quay, Bartlett, Wrightsman & Catron, 1961).

war the Harwood Manufacturing Company employed about 700 people, mostly women, to make garments. A standing policy not to hire women over 30 years old became a serious obstacle to maintaining a full production force because of the acute shortage of help. The personnel psychologist reexamined the policy in the light of his knowledge of age and productivity relationships and data he collected informally around the plant. He concluded that older women would perform as well as the younger ones.

His conclusion met with strong management resistance. Management believed that older workers produced less, were absent more, had a shorter working life and were harder to teach new skills. When management was shown high productivity figures for older women, it attributed them to exceptional situations. Argument was futile. But management finally reacted favorably to a proposal that it help plan a modest study to see how much the company was actually losing from older workers. Management also supplied the criteria of job performance that would be acceptable to it: rate of production, rate of turnover, absenteeism, and speed of learning. The employees were grouped by age (16-20, 21-25, 26-30, 31-35, over 35 years) and records were compared for the four yardsticks which management had suggested.

Findings: The over-30 groups were above average on production, the 21-25 group was especially low. The over-30 groups learned new skills faster than the others. The older groups had slightly better attendance and much lower turnover. Result: management was convinced, decided to change the policy.

Judging by his past experience, the personnel man emphasizes that management would not have changed its mind if it had not taken an active part in the study. A similar resistance to changing the policy was found among supervisors. They were won over only after a series of meetings in small groups in which they discussed the whole problem of age and productivity, and thus felt partly responsible for the change (Marrow & French, 1945).

3. Here is still further documentation from industry of the value of participation as a way of winning people over to a desired end. The setting was a company that manufactured wooden toys. One part of the process consisted of spraying paint on partially assembled toys, and then hanging them on an overhead belt of continuously moving hooks which carried the toys into a drying oven. The eight girls who did the painting sat in a line in front of the hooks. The plant engineers had calculated the speed of the belt so that a trained girl would be able to hang a freshly painted toy on each hook before it passed out of her reach. Girls were paid on a piece rate basis, determined by their performance as a group. New girls were put on a learning bonus, which decreased every month. At the end of six months, the learning bonus was cut off and the girls were on their own.

The painting operation was a management headache. High turnover, low morale, and frequent absenteeism were the symptoms. The girls complained that the hooks were moving too fast, and that the time study engineers had set the piece rates wrong. Many of the hooks were moving into the oven without toys on them.

A consultant was hired by the plant management to study the situation. After preliminary investigation, the consultant tried several times to persuade the foreman to call a meeting of the girls to discuss working conditions with them. The reluctant foreman finally agreed, and the first of several meetings was held right after the end of a shift. At the meeting, a spokesman for the girls elaborated on their complaints about the speed of the hooks. She explained that the girls could keep up with the moving hooks for short periods of time, but they purposely held back for fear that they would be expected to maintain the pace all day long. What the girls wanted was to "adjust the speed of the belt faster or slower, depending on how we feel." The foreman agreed to pass this request on to the engineers and superintendent.

As might be expected, the engineers reacted unfavorably to this proposal, and only after much persuasion did they agree to try out the idea. The foreman had a graduated control dial with points marked "low," "medium," and "fast" installed at the booth of one of the girls. The speed of the belt could now be adjusted within these limits.

Findings: The girls were delighted with this arrangement, and spent much of their free time during the first few days deciding how the speed of the belt should be varied from time to time during the day. Within a week the pattern had been established. The productivity of the group as well as their morale went up considerably. The quality of the girls' work was as satisfactory as it had been previously. And it is interesting to note that the average speed at which the girls themselves were running the belt was *higher* than the constant speed they had been complaining about.

Considering just this much of the situation, we may conclude that this is another example of the value of participation in bringing about attitude (and behavior) change. There is a postscript to this experience. The new system worked too well. The learning girls were turning out much more than they had been expected to produce when the learning bonus was established. The combination of this bonus (which was to decrease with time and not as a function of productivity) and the piece rate that the girls were now earning gave them larger earnings than those of many skilled workers in the plant. In addition, the increased production in the paint room created a pile-up at the drying oven and a vacuum in the toy-making department. To add to the trouble, the prestige of the engineers had suffered. Provoked by these repercussions in other parts of the plant, management arbitrarily and abruptly called a halt to the new system, and went back to the old way. Within a month, six of the eight girls had quit.

The obvious moral for management is that changing one part of an operation may have implications for other parts of the operation. Improvement in a local situation may not be in the best interests of the rest of the enterprise (Whyte, 1955).

4. Still another study in an industrial setting illustrates not only the value of participation, but also that different kinds of participation may show differences in their effects. The study was conducted in a midwestern garment manufacturing company which employed about a thousand people. Four small groups of employees from three different departments took part in the study. Each group met once a week for five weeks. Their output records for a period of time before the experiment started were used as a base line against which to compare the results of the study. The weekly discussions for *all* groups were oriented about employee problems, company policies, employee benefits, and community relations. An additional topic was introduced in *two* of the groups: they discussed their output record during the past week, and agreed on their output goal for the following week.

> *Findings:* An increase in production occurred for all four groups. A markedly greater increase in production, however, was found for the two groups that examined their past week's records and set new goals for the next week. No relationships were found between production increases of individual workers and factors such as their ages, length of employment,

earnings, dexterity, or intelligence (the latter two as measured by psychological tests). The authors concluded that participation in either form increased production, but that discussion plus goal-setting was superior to discussion alone (Lawrence & Smith, 1955).

Discussion

Two social scientists who have conducted studies in communication offer some likely reasons for the effectiveness of group discussion and decision over lecture methods (Katz & Lazarsfeld, 1955). One hypothesis is that the show of hands at the end makes it possible for each person present to see the willingness of other people to do something to which they had formerly been indifferent or negative.

Another hypothesis is that when you appeal to a group to change one of its norms (for example, to use certain meats they had not used before), you may be appealing to other values which are *also* part of its norms. For example, in influencing housewives to cook unpopular meats during the war, the persuaders were appealing to another set of norms: patriotism. If the propagandist can find alternative group norms to appeal to, he should have a far easier time getting the kind of change he wants.

Lastly, it is suggested that the group discussion is conducive to "talking out" the emotional insulation surrounding a given attitude. Removing this wrapper makes the group more vulnerable to the influence of a counter-proposal (Katz & Lazarsfeld, 1955). Participation means a heightened degree of involvement. However, even though group discussions generate more involvement, they do not by themselves lead to a decision. The audience may be ready to make up its mind, but the leader has a part to play in changing this readiness into action (Lewin, 1953).

With respect to the situation in the toy factory, the author suggests three explanations of why letting the girls control the speed of the moving belt made so much difference in their productivity:

(1) The girls were no longer afraid to work at top speed. They did not worry about the piece rate being changed by engineers who might happen to observe them during a period of high output.

(2) Machines operate at a constant rate. People usually do not. Once the girls had decided at what times of the day they wanted to work faster, and at what times slower, they tended to stick to the same daily pattern. In effect they were adjusting the machine to a

human rhythm instead of having to adjust themselves to the machine.

(3) No normal person is happy in a situation that he cannot control to some extent. This is an explanation not only of what happened in the toy factory, but also of the effectiveness of group discussion generally. Group discussions can give the participants a voice in their future. The value of a discussion lies in the knowledge that each person's ideas will receive consideration even though every idea may not be incorporated into a plan of action. In industry, for example, employees may at first respond favorably to group discussions because of the novelty of being asked their opinions. In the long run, however, the beneficial effect on the participants would be likely to continue only if some of their suggestions were put into use (Whyte, 1955).

Suggested Readings: Group Discussion

(1) Lewin, K. Studies in group decision. In Cartwright and Zander, *Group dynamics.* Evanston: Row, Peterson, 1953.

4

THE PERSISTENCE OF OPINION CHANGE

Does propaganda have a lasting influence on opinions?

Is opinion change at its highest point right after the persuasive communication has ended?

Are there any ways to make the impact of a persuasive appeal last longer?

In time the effects of a persuasive communication tend to wear off.

In the typical attitude change study, an individual's opinion on a specific topic is assessed. This assessment is then followed by his exposure to a persuasive communication designed to change that opinion. Finally, the subject's opinion is re-assessed to see if the persuasive appeal has had any effect. Oftentimes it has. But for how long? Will a man persuaded today remain persuaded tomorrow? Do the effects of persuasive appeals wear off with passing time? These questions were asked by two investigators, William Watts and William McGuire, in 1964.

Specimen studies

1. In their experiment Watts and McGuire measured persistence of induced opinion change and retention of persuasive communications in 191 undergraduates. Every subject was exposed to four persuasive appeals, each pre-tested to determine in advance what student opinion on the topic would be. The four issues selected were: "Puerto Rico should be admitted to the union as the 51st state"; "Courts should deal more leniently with juvenile delinquents"; "The Secretary of State should be elected by the people, not appointed by the President"; and "The state sales tax should be abolished." Opinion change was measured on a 15-point scale where subjects could register their level of agreement-disagreement with the contents of the persuasive communications. Recall was assessed by ascertaining the subject's ability to recollect and recognize various aspects of the four persuasive appeals. The total experiment lasted six weeks, with subjects attending four separate sessions. Recall and opinion change measures were administered once during the study—at the conclusion of the fourth experimental session. What were the results of the investigation?

Findings: There were three major findings of interest: (1) Opinion change was most evident immediately after exposure to the persuasive appeal. With the passage of time the impact of the communication steadily decreased, as reflected in the decay of the initial opinion change; (2) The subject's ability to recall and recognize the contents of persuasive appeals also decreased with the passage of time; (3) At first, opinion change was positively related to recollection of the persuasive communications: the more remembered, the more the change. With the passage of time, however, this relationship weakened to a point where sometimes message recall was *negatively* related to opinion change (the less one recalled of the persuasive appeal the more he was persuaded!). Thus, it seems that the effects of a persuasive appeal "wear off" with passing time, as does the individual's ability to recall and recognize the contents of that appeal (Watts & McGuire, 1964).

2. In a cross-cultural study, James Whittaker and Robert Meade (1968) examined the longevity of opinion change in university students from Brazil, Hong Kong, Lebanon, Rhodesia, and India. In the first phase of the study all subjects filled out an opinion questionnaire designed to assess their opinions on certain issues (they were asked to express the extent of their agreement or disagreement with such statements as: "We should continue supporting the United Nations" and "A cancer cure will be found within the next five years"). The students were also asked to select from a list containing "classes of people" (e.g., lawyers, ministers, engineers, professors, etc.) those they thought to be "authority groups" whose opinions they would most respect and those groups whose opinions they would least respect. The second phase of the investigation involved deception by the experimenter. Each subject was re-administered the opinion questionnaire. This time, however, he was provided with a "comparison set of answers" for each issue. Unknown to the subject, these "comparison answers" were determined by the experimenter, based on the subject's response to the first opinion questionnaire. Each comparison answer was divergent from the subject's initial position. Further, on one-third of the issues, the comparison answers were attributed to members of the subject's "high authority" group; on another third to "low authority group" members; and on the remaining third, the responses were credited to the "majority of students at this college."

In the final phase of the study (one month later) students filled out the opinion questionnaire for a third time. This time no authority groups were indicated. Of interest in this investigation was the longevity of opinion change as a function of source credibility (the impact of "high" and "low" authority references on subject's opinions).

Findings: The results indicate that "differential source credibility produces differences in opinion change regardless of

the culture involved. High credible sources in general produce greater opinion change than low credible sources."
*Further, opinion change decayed over time regardless of
whether a high or low credible source was involved.* In other
words, there was less opinion change on the third questionnaire than on the second no matter which credibility condition
the subject experienced (Whittaker & Meade, 1968).*

3. Both affirmative and negative speeches were prepared on two
propositions: (1) the federal government should make medical care
available to all people; (2) the government should require federal
arbitration of labor disputes. The speeches were judged for effectiveness by speech professors, and then rewritten until they were all
rated equally effective. The final form of each speech was tape-
recorded for later use.

Over a thousand students in several groups took part in the experiment. First, they indicated their attitudes on one of the propositions on a questionnaire form. Then they listened to either the
affirmative or the negative speech on that proposition, and then
answered more attitude questions. Thirty days later, they filled out
a third attitude questionnaire on the topic. A control group also
filled out questionnaires when the other students did, but were not
exposed to any of the recorded speeches.

> *Findings:* Each speech had a strong, immediate effect on the
> students' attitudes in the expected direction. The negative
> speeches produced a greater change than the positive speeches.
>
> After thirty days, the attitudes of all of the students had
> moved back toward their original positions. But the influence
> of the speeches was still evident. About one-third of the
> effect of the affirmative speeches was still measurable, as was
> about two-thirds of the effect of the negative speeches. The
> author drew two conclusions from his data: (1) after thirty
> days the influence of a message is weaker than right after its
> presentation, but there still is some influence; (2) the stronger
> the immediate effectiveness of the message, the greater will
> be its influence after thirty days (Cromwell, 1955).

4. The question of how long a communication will be remembered
has something to do with whether or not the audience believes it

---

* See also: Cook, T., & Insko, C. Persistence of attitude change as a function
of conclusion reexposure: A laboratory-field experiment. *Journal of Personality
and Social Psychology,* 1968, *9,* 322–328.

and is favorably disposed toward it. One social scientist started with these hypotheses: The stronger the belief that a statement is true, the longer it will be remembered; the stronger the belief that it is false, the sooner it will be forgotten. The more highly approved a statement is, the longer it will be remembered; the more disapproved it is, the sooner it will be forgotten.

A group of 200 college students were handed a list of pro-Russian and anti-Russian statements. For example, one statement was "Equality is given to all racial and minority groups in Russia." The students indicated on a questionnaire whether they believed each statement to be true or false. They also showed whether they approved or disapproved of the general idea of the statement. For example, should all racial and minority groups in any country be accorded equal treatment with everyone else.

The statements in the questionnaire were woven into an essay, "Russia Today." Starting a week after the initial questionnaires were filled out, the essay was read to the students once every other day for a total of five readings. Memory tests on the essay were given immediately after the last reading, and every two weeks thereafter for two months.

> *Findings:* Believing statements to be true increases the chance that they will be remembered; but believing that they are false does *not* seem to make them more easily forgotten. Attitudes seem to work the same way: approving a statement increased the chance that it would be remembered, but disapproving it did not have much effect in the other direction. When a person both believes *and* approves of something, it has the best chance of being remembered. When both disbelief and disapproval are working at the same time, the chances of forgetting are greatest. Finally, when a person believes something but does not approve of it, or approves of it but does not believe it, stronger influence on remembering is exerted by the degree of approval, rather than by the degree of belief (Garber, 1955).

Discussion

There is no conclusive evidence on how long a changed opinion stays that way. Some investigators have reported examples of opinion change that lasted for years. Others are more likely to agree with an authority who wrote: "In those rare instances when educators, propagandists, advertisers, and others who want to influence large numbers of people have bothered to make an objective evaluation of the enduring changes produced by their efforts, they have been able to demonstrate only the most negligible effects " (Cartwright, 1951).

Why the disagreement between authorities on the longevity of changed opinions? Actually, the "short-term" and "long-term" advocates are both right—sometimes changed opinions are short-lived, other times, seemingly indestructible: the problem lies in distinguishing the types of opinions that are changed and the procedures for changing them. Generally, opinions that are meaningful (important) to the individual and/or have been established through long-term (or intensive) persuasive efforts are relatively stable and unlikely to change; opinions that are not of central concern to the person and/or have been changed in the course of "one-shot" or limited persuasive appeals are relatively unstable and open to modification. In the typical laboratory manipulation of opinions, where the subject matter is not often involving to subjects and the persuasive appeals are not emphatic, long-term attitude change should be the *exception,* not the rule. * On the other hand, opinions are quite resistant to decay when they have been formed through extensive persuasive efforts (e.g., Carron, 1964). Such is often the case with opinions established during long-term psychotherapy.

Suggested Readings: Persistence of Opinion Change

(1) Watts, W. A., & McGuire, W. J. Persistence of induced opinion change and retention of the inducing message contents. *Journal of Abnormal and Social Psychology,* 1964, *68,* 233-241.

(2) Whittaker, J., & Meade, R. Retention of opinion change as a function of differential source credibility: A cross-cultural study. *International Journal of Psychology,* 1968, *3,* 103-108.

---

* This point has been effectively presented by Hovland (1959). An elaboration at what he said is presented in the section on "Social Science Methods." See Chapter 8.

More of the desired opinion change may be measurable some time after exposure to the communication than right after exposure (the "sleeper effect").

Specimen studies

1. One in the series of *Why We Fight* movies used during World War II was called the "Battle of Britain," made to give U.S. troops confidence in our British ally. A questionnaire asking for opinions about Britain was completed by ten infantry training companies, after which five of them saw the film, and five of them were used as a control group and did not see the film. Five days after the picture was shown, about half of the men who saw it, and half of those who did not, filled out a questionnaire containing both opinion items and factual questions about Britain. Nine weeks later, the other half of each group filled out the same questionnaire. In the results, the responses after five days were compared with the responses after nine weeks.

> *Findings:* The factual material suffered with time. More was forgotten after nine weeks than after five days. But interestingly enough, some of the opinion responses were *more* in the desired direction after nine weeks than after five days, while the rest of the opinion responses showed the expected decrease in desired change. The authors named their special finding "the sleeper effect" (Hovland, Lumsdaine & Sheffield, 1949).

2. The sleeper effect was studied in an experiment on some high school students who were exposed to a communication on the effects of smoking. A feature of this experiment was a discounting statement: after the communication, one of the groups was told that evidence on the effects of smoking is by no means complete, and we are learning new facts every day. The experimenter's hypothesis was that the group that heard this discounting treatment should show less of the intended opinion change right after exposure than the other group, but show the *same* amount of change in the long run, after the discounting effect had worn off. Opinion measurements were made before exposure, right after exposure, and three and again six weeks later.

Findings: The group that heard the discounting statement and the group that did not were more alike in extent of opinion change later on than they were immediately after exposure. Thus, the sleeper effect showed itself again, even though the results were not quite as marked as they were in the earlier experiments (Weiss, 1953).

Discussion

A sleeper effect is said to occur when there is more measurable opinion change in the desired direction some time following exposure compared with that immediately following exposure. Several experiments have turned up sleeper effects in different situations. In addition to the two reported here, we can include those described in the chapter on characteristics of the communicator (persuader). These experiments made use of high and low credibility communicators, and their results indicate that opinion right after exposure favors the high credibility source, but that these effects wear off in a few weeks. Eventually there was almost the same amount of opinion change regardless of whether the subjects were initially exposed to the high or the low credibility communicator (Hovland & Weiss, 1951; Kelman & Hovland, 1953).[*]

The authors of the first experiment reported here (the one on the Battle of Britain film) concluded that changes of opinion of a general rather than a specific nature may be more likely to show a sleeper effect. They feel that a sleeper effect is more likely to occur among people who are already predisposed to accept an opinion; possibly because their motivation for wanting to change their opinions will have something to feed on after they have been exposed to the communication (Hovland, Lumsdaine & Sheffield, 1949). Related to this is another very real possibility: Once the topic has been presented, the audience pays more attention to what is said about it in the mass media. This heightened awareness may lead to more reading and listening and thinking about it, until an opinion has been formed (Hovland, Janis & Kelley, 1953).

There are some concepts in the psychology of memory that were useful to the author of the second experiment reported here (the one on the effects of smoking). His hypothesis, which the data supported, was that the "discounting" statement would wear off some time after the audience was exposed to the communication. What is im-

---

[*] For a more detailed description of these studies and a discussion of their results, see pp. 110-111 and 113-114.

plied is that immediately after exposure, the emergence of an opinion change would be *actively prevented* by the effects of the discounting statement. But because so much more emphasis was given to the presentation on smoking than to the discounting statement (about the incompleteness of the evidence on smoking), the struggle between the emerging opinion and the inhibiting discounting statement would eventually be resolved in favor of the opinion change. These ideas tie in with the concept that forgetting is an active process: something else interferes with a thing learned. Forgetting is not always just the disappearance of a thought from the mind.

This concept of the sleeper effect, even before it is fully explored, may have significant implications for anyone who is interested in estimating the effects of a particular communication. The elapsed time between the actual communication and the measuring of its effects takes on a new meaning. In summary, it is safe to say that something like a sleeper effect has been repeatedly demonstrated.[*] Finding out more about how it works and how to interpret data in the light of the relationships it implies is a task which is still being explored.

Suggested Readings: The Sleeper Effect

(1) Weiss, W. A "sleeper" effect in opinion change. *Journal of Abnormal and Social Psychology*, 1953, *48*, 173-180.

---

[*] Whittaker and Meade failed to confirm the sleeper effect in their experiment described in Specimen Study 2, p. 71 (Whittaker & Meade, 1968). The majority of studies, however, have supported the phenomenon. In the Lewin (1953) investigation it was found that a housewife's willingness to serve unpopular meats was greater not immediately after group discussion but three weeks later.

Opinion change is more persistent over a period of time if the persuasive appeal is: (1) repeated and/or (2) requires active (rather than passive) listener participation.

How to prolong the impact of a persuasive appeal: now there's a problem Madison Avenue can appreciate! Convincing Jane Doe to purchase a "Brand X" refrigerator is useless if, by the time she visits the store, the effect of the persuasive appeal has worn off. Advertisers have employed many types of persuasive appeals in an effort to sustain changed opinions. They have discovered, long before psychologists, that repeating a communication tends to prolong its influence. Specimen Studies 1 and 2 below attest to the effectiveness of message repetition for prolonging opinion change and lend credence to an old advertising motto: "To keep selling, keep reminding." Or, brought up to date: "Repetition sells good; like an ad campaign should."

Specimen studies

1. Let us assume you were bent on discovering a way to prolong the impact of a persuasive communication. You enlist the aid of several hundred undergraduates and expose them to a persuasive appeal arguing for election of the President by Congress instead of by the voters. Later you send the students postcards requesting their attendance at a second session. On one-half of the postcards you also mention the topic of the earlier persuasive appeal (congressional election of the President). During the second session you examine the success of your persuasive appeal by asking the subjects to indicate on an 11-point scale: "How much do you agree or disagree that the President should be elected by Congress?" You are interested in discovering whether subjects given communication reexposure (postcards stating the topic of the persuasive appeal) will exhibit more opinion change (favorability toward Congressional election of the President) than subjects receiving no such communication repetition. What would you find? Well—for a starter—that the experiment had already been performed by Thomas Cook and Chester Insko in 1968! What, then, did they discover?

Findings: Although the impact of the persuasive appeal decreased for all subjects with the passage of time—reexposure produced a greater persistence effect than did no reexposure (Cook & Insko, 1968). *

2. Affirmative and negative speeches were prepared on the topics of socialized medicine and federal aid to education. The two versions of each speech were submitted to speech professors who judged them for effectiveness. The speeches were rewritten and rejudged a number of times until they were all rated as about equally effective. Each speech was then tape-recorded for later use.

Several groups of students, over 200 in all, took part in the experiment. They were told that a study was being made of some of the problems of public speaking and audience reactions to speeches. The students then answered a number of questions to determine their attitudes on socialized medicine and federal aid to education. As soon as the questionnaires had been collected, each group of students heard one of the tape-recorded speeches (either pro or con on one of the two topics). Lastly, they filled out another form of the attitude questionnaire on the same two topics. Thirty days later, exactly the same procedure was followed with the same students: attitude questionnaire, same speech they heard before, alternate form of questionnaire.

Findings: The questionnaires administered directly after each speech showed a shift in opinion in the expected direction. The attitude questionnaire that was administered just before the second exposure to the speech showed that after thirty days had passed, some of the opinion change caused by the first exposure to the speech had worn off. The measurement made following the second exposure to the speech revealed two things: (1) students were not influenced as much by the speech the second time they heard it as they had been the first time; (2) the second presentation brought the level of attitude change up to what it had been immediately after the first presentation, thirty days previously (Cromwell & Kunkel, 1952).

Discussion

Early in the history of modern psychology, just as today, there was much experimental activity directed to the study of human mem-

---

* See also: Wilson, W., & Miller, H. Repetition, order of presentation, timing of arguments and measures as determinants of opinion change. *Journal of Personality and Social Psychology*, 1968, *9*, 184–188.

ory and forgetting. Some of the findings of those earlier psychologists about the processes of forgetting are valid to this day. One is that people do not forget what they read or hear in equal increments. An audience that has been exposed to a persuasive message will not forget 10% of what they heard each week for ten weeks until they have forgotten the message. Instead, the audience will forget most of what they heard after two or three days. Then, the little they still retain gradually dwindles down to a few fragments of what they had originally heard. Interestingly enough, these last bits of material are often remembered for quite some time.

Advertisers can make use of the known pattern of forgetting. For instance, a direct mail campaign whose timing is one mailing a week for six weeks might not have the impact of a campaign which consists of three mailings in close succession. When the follow-ups are sent soon after the first mailing, the advertiser is catching his audience before they have forgotten most of what they read in the preceding mailing. The impact of the first mailing is being strengthened before nearly all of it is forgotten.

We do not have to look far—about as far as the living room TV set—for evidence that persuasion by repetition has an army of proponents. But what about the use of "active participation" to prolong the impact of a persuasive appeal? We have encountered "active participation" in two earlier contexts and are already familiar with its role in changing opinions. On pages 19-21 we observed that the impact of a persuasive appeal is enhanced by requiring active, rather than passive, participation by the listener. Then, on pages 62-67 we concluded that active audience participation (group discussion and decision-making) helps to overcome resistance. Thus, it has already been determined that active participation can enhance the effectiveness of persuasive appeals. What will be documented here is the long-term impact (persistence) of that effectiveness.

One of the best examples of how active participation can maintain an opinion once it has been formed or changed was provided by Watts in 1967. In his experiment,* 140 university students were divided into six experimental groups that either read (passive participation) or wrote (active participation) about one of three possible issues. A questionnaire designed to assess opinions on the three topics was administered to students just after they had read or written about the issues and again six weeks later. In the second

---

* A more detailed presentation of this study appears as Specimen Study 1 (page 19).

testing session student involvement with, and recall of, the issues was also tested.

In examining his data, Watts found that initially both active and passive participation led to significant opinion change. Thus, students who either read or wrote a persuasive appeal favoring a specified issue changed their opinions in the desired direction. But what about persistence of opinion change? In the follow-up testing session six weeks later, subjects who had composed persuasive appeals (active participation) displayed significantly greater persistence of the initially induced opinion change than students who had read the persuasive communication (passive participation). In this study, active participation was clearly superior to passive participation in long-term opinion change (Watts, 1967). *

The knowledge that active participation prolongs opinion change finds practical application in psychotherapy. The increasing popularity and success of the newer "role playing" and "psychodrama" therapies with their emphasis on active patient involvement in the treatment process is their way of recognizing the doctrine of "active participation."

The importance of active participation in long-range opinion change has also been documented with T-groups (Carron, 1964) and reference groups (Newcomb, 1963). Currently, active participation is being emphasized and practiced by an ever widening circle of individuals and groups in this society. VISTA, Peace Corps, Black Panthers, Peace Marchers, campus demonstrators, sensitivity training groups—all emphasize activities that center on participation. The implications of these movements for society have yet to be determined—possibly the study of active participation might provide us with some insights.

Suggested Readings: Prolonging Opinion Change

(1) Carron, T. Human relations training and attitude change: A vector analysis. *Personnel Psychology,* 1964, *17,* 403-424.
(2) Cook, T., & Insko, C. Persistence of attitude change as a function of conclusion reexposure: A laboratory-field experiment. *Journal of Personality and Social Psychology,* 1968, *9,* 322-328.

---

* For another example of how active participation affects the persistence of attitude change see: Mitnick, L. & McGinnies, E. Influencing ethnocentrism in small discussion groups through a film communication. *Journal of Abnormal and Social Psychology,* 1958, *56,* 82–90.

(3) Newcomb, T. Persistence and regression of changed attitudes: Long-range studies. *Journal of Social Issues,* 1963, *19,* 3-14.
(4) Watts, W. Relative persistence of opinion change induced by active compared to passive participation. *Journal of Personality and Social Psychology,* 1967, *5,* 4-15.

5

THE AUDIENCE AS INDIVIDUALS

When you talk, who do you think is listening?

Who is more persuasible, a man or a woman?

In order to change someone's opinion, what must you know about his reasons for holding that opinion?

Does knowing about someone's personality help you determine his susceptibility to persuasive appeals?

The people you may want most in your audience are often least likely to be there.

Let us assume you were a political candidate running on the Republican ticket for office. During your campaign you decide to give a series of speeches presenting your platform. What segment of the voter constituency do you think will show up to hear your address? If you guessed "mostly Democrats" you'd be wrong. You would find mostly Republicans, not Democrats or Independents, listening to Republican campaign speeches. An early investigation designed to locate the influences which determine voter preferences showed that people read the papers and listen to the speeches that support their own points of view (Lazarsfeld, Berelson, & Gaudet, 1944).

This "selective exposure" hypothesis—that people tend to expose themselves only to persuasive appeals with which they already agree—has been repeatedly supported in a wide variety of experimental settings (as the following specimen studies indicate).*

Specimen studies

1. On April 7, 1965 Lyndon Johnson made a major foreign policy speech at Johns Hopkins University. It was widely known in advance that the address would be supportive of the government's military policy in Vietnam. Prior to the speech, 187 first-year psychology students filled out an opinion questionnaire designed to assess attitudes toward the government's military policy in Vietnam. Two days after the president's address the students filled out the questionnaire a second time. They were also asked if they: " (a) had actually seen or heard the president's speech, (b) knew indirectly about the speech, or (c) had neither heard the speech nor learned anything about it afterward." The experimenters hypothesized that students who supported the government's position on Vietnam would have been more likely to attend President Johnson's speech (which was congruent with their beliefs) than those students who were less favorable toward such a stand.

---

* The "selective exposure" hypothesis has also been supported in studies by Brock & Becker (1965) and Mills (1965). Such research findings have been used to support the "cognitive dissonance" theory of Leon Festinger. (See Cohen, 1964; Festinger, 1962, 1964; Lawrence & Festinger, 1962; Zimbardo, 1969).

Findings: The hypothesis was supported. "Among the females, * those who were inclined to support a firm stand in Vietnam were more likely to expose themselves to a communication in which it was evident that such a policy would be defended. Those female subjects who were only lukewarm in their support of such a policy were less inclined to attend either directly or indirectly to the President's talk" (McGinnies & Rosenbaum, 1965).

2. Some cross-cultural validation for the "selective exposure" hypothesis is provided by Lutfy Diab in his study of 260 Arab students. Psychologist Diab suspected that an individual's political views would influence his exposure to the mass media, specifically, that a person would read newspapers and listen to radio stations that supported his point of view to the exclusion of media expressing opposite points of view.

To test his assumption Diab analyzed questionnaire data from his students which revealed: (a) the newspapers and radio stations they preferred; (b) their position regarding Arab unity. Prior to examining the questionnaires, Diab had a panel of judges categorize all Arab Middle East newspapers and radio stations according to their pro- or anti-position on Arab unity. With this information Diab was in a position to see if a person's attitude on Arab unity had a bearing on his approach to the mass media.

Findings: In general, the results support the selective exposure hypothesis. Subjects who were firmly pro- or anti-Arab unity showed preferences for newspapers and radio stations expressing points of view similar to their own. Thus, as in the McGinnies and Rosenbaum study (Specimen Study 1 on p. 84), individuals exposed themselves to sources of information congruent with their own beliefs (Diab, 1965).

3. It is reasonable to assume that most advertisers are at least as (if not more) interested in reaching people who do not use their products as they are in reaching those who do. Some information on whom the ads do reach came out of an experiment designed to test this hypothesis: that *after making a decision,* people tend to look for information that supports their decision and to avoid informa-

---

* Initial male attitudes on Vietnam were too homogeneous to allow for selective exposure to operate.

tion that conflicts with it. The hypothesis was tested by studying the readership of automobile advertisements—owners of new cars and owners of older cars. Specifically, these three propositions on car ad readership were formulated:

(1) New car owners will read advertisements for their own cars more often than ads for cars which they considered but did not buy, or ads for other cars which they did not consider at all.

(2) New car owners will read ads for cars they considered seriously but did not buy even less often than ads for cars they did not consider at all. (This hypothesis is in line with the idea that, after making a decision, people avoid information that conflicts with their decision.)

(3) Owners of old cars will not have these patterns of readership, because the effects of a decision wear off with time.

Names of men who had recently purchased new cars were taken from a state registration list. The same list provided names of owners of old cars, cars manufactured several years before the study was made. Interviews were conducted with 65 new car owners and 60 old car owners. The car owners were told that the survey had to do with advertising. There was no mention of the real purpose of the study. As part of the interview, the respondents were asked about the magazines they read, and how thoroughly they read each one. After remembering what they could about the ads they had seen, respondents went through actual copies of the magazines and indicated the extent to which they had read each of the automobile ads. There were a number of other questions in the same vein.

Findings: New car owners read ads for their own make of car more often than ads for any other make (support for the first hypothesis). Old car owners did not read ads for their make of car any more often than they read ads for other cars (support for the third hypothesis). New car owners did *not* read fewer ads for cars which they considered seriously but did not buy as compared with cars that they did not consider at all (refutation of the second hypothesis). The authors offer a possible explanation for the result which was contrary to the second hypothesis. Perhaps new car owners read ads for cars which they considered and then rejected in order to look for disadvantages in these rejected cars and thus reassure themselves of the wisdom of their decisions (Ehrlich, Guttman, Schonbach & Mills, 1957).

4. Before leaving the topic of "selective exposure," one related issue seems worthy of examination. We have established that a person tends to expose himself only to persuasive appeals with which he already agrees. However, what if an individual encounters a presentation where both his and an opposing point of view are aired?

A study by Hans Sebald (1962) gives us some insight into this question. In this investigation 152 Ohio State University students who had watched the 1960 Kennedy-Nixon presidential debates filled out questionnaires designed to "assess their attitudes or changes of attitudes toward the two presidential candidates before and after their . . . debates." Here, then, is a situation in which an individual is exposed to two different viewpoints, one of which he supports and the other of which he opposes. What happens?

Findings: According to the Sebald results, a form of "selective exposure" also occurs in these circumstances. The individual attends to those segments of the communication that support his views (selective perception); perceives and recalls information only if it reinforces his prior images (selective memory); and distorts statements to eliminate dissonant material (selective distortion). In short, the listener hears what he wants to hear, based on his prior attitudes and beliefs. In the Sebald investigation this meant that the TV viewer took from the Kennedy-Nixon debates information that preserved " (1) a favorable image of the candidate of the preferred party; and (2) an unfavorable image of the candidate of the opposing party" (Sebald, 1962).

Discussion

It seems that persuasive appeals, before they can effect opinion change, must first overcome a host of individual defenses, including selective exposure, selective perception, selective memory and selective distortion. If the Red Cross advertised a free booklet telling about the blood donor program and what it has meant in time of emergency, many of the requests for it might be expected to come from the small fraction of our citizens who have already given their blood, whereas the Red Cross, of course, would be most interested in reaching non-donors. A frequent complaint in parent-teacher associations is that the meetings are attended by parents of good students. The parents of poor students, for whom the meetings are often planned, rarely attend. A large number of such illustrations could be found to show that people look for the **programs, articles** and news items that support their attitudes and beliefs, and tend not to expose themselves to communications which conflict with their own viewpoints.* And the support, once found, need not be laced with too many facts! In the words of one author: ". . . many people may accept something they *want* to accept as 'proved' by the flimsiest of evidence: the mere invoking of emotional appeals ('Gentlemen of the jury, this woman is a mother'), the introduction of absolute irrelevancies ('Fascism is OK because Mussolini made the trains run on time') or the shallowest false logic or syllogistic reasoning ('No cat has eight tails. Every cat has one more tail than no cat. Every cat has nine tails') " (Miller, 1946).

Suggested Readings: Selective Exposure

(1) Diab, L. Studies in social attitudes: II. Selectivity in mass communication media as a function of attitude-medium discrepancy. *The Journal of Social Psychology,* 1965, *67*, 297-302.

(2) McGinnies, E. & Rosenbaum, L. A test of the selective-exposure hypothesis in persuasion. *The Journal of Social Psychology,* 1965, *61*, 237-240.

(3) Sebald, H. Limitations of communication: Mechanisms of image maintenance in form of selective perception, selective memory and selective distortion. *Journal of Communication,* 1962, *12*, 142-149.

---

* For a good discussion of this topic see Jones and Gerard (1967), pp. 194–211.

In our society, women are more persuasible than men.

In America who do you think are more persuasible: men or women? Your answer would probably depend on many factors, such as pride, marital status, nearness of mother-in-law, and your adroitness with the opposite sex! Is man the seducer? Is every woman an Eve or a Delilah? Psychological investigations provide us with a surprisingly decisive answer: in experiment after experiment the fair sex is the more easily persuaded. * This is one of the most consistent and reliable findings in the field of persuasion.

Specimen studies

1. Consider, for example, an experiment by Thomas Scheidel (1963). 104 male and 138 female college students were given an attitude survey designed to assess opinions on the expansion of federal powers, followed by an eleven minute persuasive communication opposing further expansion of federal power in the areas of health and education. Immediately after hearing the persuasive appeal, students filled out an alternate form of the attitude survey administered earlier. Scheidel wanted to know if attitude change in this situation would be different for males and females (would women be more swayed by the anti-federal power speech than men?).

> *Findings:* "Women were found to be significantly more persuasible than men." That is, they were influenced to a greater degree by the 11-minute persuasive appeal, as reflected in their opinion shift on the second attitude survey. Further, women (more than men) exhibited a greater "generalization of conformity" by becoming generally more negative toward the expansion of federal power, even in areas not specifically mentioned in the persuasive communication (Scheidel, 1963) **

2. If a subject is asked to view a stationary light point in an otherwise darkened room it will appear to move slightly. This illusion,

---

* See, for example, Carrigan & Julian, 1966; Janis & Field, 1958; King, 1958; Reitan & Shaw, 1964; Scheidel, 1963; and Whittaker, 1965.
** This tendency for females to generalize more readily than men has also been noted by Allen and Crutchfield (1963) in their study of conformity.

known as the autokinetic phenomenon, was used by James Whittaker to study sex differences in susceptibility to interpersonal persuasion. First he tested 20 undergraduates (10 male; 10 female) individually in the autokinetic situation. Each subject was asked to make judgments as to how far the light point "moved" over several trials. "Under such conditions, subjects establish a standard of judgment that is maintained under similar conditions in subsequent sessions." Once each subject's range of judgments was known, Whittaker was ready for the second phase of his investigation. Each student was re-tested in the autokinetic situation; this time, however, with a partner who (unknown to the subject) was in "cahoots" with the experimenter. This "partner" was instructed to make judgments that were variant from those expressed by the subject in his first experimental session. Would the subject stick to the judgments he had standardized in the first experimental session or would he modify his estimates (be persuaded) to conform with those made by his (her) "partner"?

> *Findings:* Female subjects were significantly more persuasible than males in the autokinetic situation, revising their estimates more frequently to conform to the "doctored" judgments of their "partner." Further, all subjects (regardless of sex) were persuaded to a greater degree when paired with male (as opposed to female) "partners." Evaluating this finding, Dr. Whittaker speculated that ". . . It is possible that male sources are generally more persuasive than female sources, regardless of the issue involved or the media employed. In broadcasting that is designed to persuade, and when the sex of the speaker is clearly apparent, the male commentator may be specifically more effective than the female" (Whittaker, 1965).

Discussion

In evaluating the findings of sex differences in persuasibility, the following points should be remembered:

(1) There is no evidence indicating that female persuasibility is a function of dispositional (physiological) factors. Most likely, such increased readiness to conform, "give in," acquiesce, etc. is the result of child training and cultural expectations which, in America, reinforce women to act submissively. As the American

female progresses in her battle for equal rights with men, we should expect sex differences in persuasibility to diminish and eventually disappear.

(2) When we speak of "women being more persuasible than men" we are referring to the "average" woman. This does not mean that *all* women are more easily swayed than men. There is overlap between the sexes as far as susceptibility to persuasion is concerned—with some females being less persuasible than males and vice versa.

(3) Finally, it should be noted that data supporting sex differences in persuasibility come from laboratory studies which deal with issues of minor relevance to the participants. A woman swayed in a psychological experiment is not necessarily as easily swayed in the "real-world" where more ego-involving, important issues are involved.* To put it another way: could the same male who persuaded a female in the autokinetic situation also convince her to go to bed with him? We suspect not as easily nor as often!

Suggested Readings: Sex and Persuasibility

(1) Scheidel, T. Sex and persuasibility. *Speech Monographs,* 1963, *30,* 353-358.
(2) Whittaker, J. Sex differences and susceptibility to interpersonal persuasion. *Journal of Social Psychology,* 1965, *66,* 91-94.

---

*A study by Carment (1968) indicates that male persuasion is ineffective in changing women's opinions on subjects they feel strongly about.

Successful persuasion takes into account the reasons underlying attitudes as well as the attitudes themselves.

Because much of our behavior can be related to our attitudes, attitudes themselves are sometimes mistaken for the fundamental causes of behavior. Some remarks of social scientists in this regard are worth summarizing (Katz, 1960; Sarnoff & Katz, 1954). Identical attitudes may have different motivational bases. Successful propaganda comes from knowing what is *behind* the attitude. For example, we might find three people who all say they are against private ownership of industry. One of them feels that way because he has only been exposed to one side of the story and has nothing else on which to base his opinion. The way to change this man's opinion may be to expose him to facts, take him to visit some factories, meet some workers and supervisors. A second person is against private ownership because that is the prevailing norm or social climate in the circles in which he finds himself. His attitudes are caused by his being a part of a group and conforming to its standards. You cannot change this fellow just by showing him facts. The facts must be presented in an atmosphere which suggests a social reward for changing his opinion. Some kind of status appeal might be a start in that direction. A third person may have negative attitudes toward private industry because by making business the scapegoat for all of his troubles, he can unload his pent-up feelings of bitterness and disappointment at the world for not giving him a better break. Attitudes often exist because they give people somebody or something to blame, instead of having to blame themselves for their own failures and shortcomings. Trying to change this third person with facts may actually do more harm than good. The more the evidence shows him how wrong he is, the more he looks for good reasons to support his beliefs. This kind of person can sometimes be influenced by helping him understand why he has a particular attitude. Once he realizes that his attitudes are protective devices for his personality, he may not hang on to them as tenaciously as before and may begin to see things in proper perspective.

In summary, three of the reasons why a man may have a particular set of attitudes are these:

(1) Factual—the attitudes help give meaning to many otherwise unrelated bits of information. These attitudes should be especially

susceptible to change by exposing the individual to new facts so that he can see things in a different light.

(2) Social—having the attitudes makes it possible for a man to feel himself acceptable to the groups of people with whom he wants to associate. He may never actually be a part of these desirable groups, but he feels closer to them by having something in common with them. Buying a certain brand of whiskey may be the only link that an individual has with men of distinction, but he may regard it as better than no link at all. Likewise, our feelings of kinship with certain social groups often underlie our attitudes toward labor unions, the United Nations, scandal magazines and so on. Attempts at changing socially derived attitudes should be most successful when they are made with reference to the acceptability of the new attitudes to the groups that are important to the audience.

(3) Personal—the attitudes provide a rationalization for an individual's shortcomings, and make it possible for him to face the world and himself. The employee who craves recognition for his achievements but doesn't receive it often cannot admit to himself that perhaps his achievements are not worthy of recognition. It may be much more satisfying for him to believe that other people are not intelligent enough to appreciate his worth. This kind of attitude is ego-defensive in function.

Specimen studies

1. A test of the hypothesis that the motivations underlying attitudes are factual, social, or personal (ego-defensive) would involve (1) being able to identify these motivations in people; (2) attempting to change some attitudes by techniques which appeal to one or more of these underlying motivations; (3) seeing if an appeal that is geared to a specific motivation works better than an appeal that is not related to the individual's motivations. Some experiments along this line have been conducted.

An experiment by Katz, Sarnoff and McClintock (1956) studied attitudes toward Negroes. A major hypothesis was that people's anti-Negro attitudes which have a personal' (ego-defensive) basis can be influenced by showing that the attitudes exist to protect the personality rather than because the facts about Negroes logically support such attitudes. Another side of the hypothesis is that people whose anti-Negro prejudice does *not* have a personal (ego-defensive) basis can be influenced more readily by presenting them with factual information about Negroes.

Accordingly, the experimenters prepared two kinds of influence materials. One was for the ego-defensive group. It explained how scapegoating works, and how anti-minority attitudes are often the result of personality conflicts that have nothing to do with the attitudes themselves. This explanation was followed by a case history of a college girl which showed the connection between her prejudices and her personality. The other kind of influence material was for the non-ego-defensive group: a resume of the achievements of Negroes in America and how they have made good whenever opportunities were available to them.

Nearly 250 college students participated in the study. At a first session, they filled out questionnaires designed to reveal their attitudes toward Negroes and took some psychological tests which helped categorize the motivations underlying their attitudes as personal (ego-defensive) or factual.

For the second session, held a week later, the students were assigned to three groups, without regard to the answers they had given the previous week. One group read the material which explained the relationship between attitudes and personality. A second group read the informational material. The third group was a control group and read nothing. After exposure to their respective reading matter, the first two groups filled out the attitude questionnaires again. The control group did likewise. Six weeks later, all three groups once more answered an attitude-toward-Negroes questionnaire.

> *Findings:* The ego-defensive people in general did respond better to the material that attempted to help them understand themselves than to the purely informational material. But as the experimenters had predicted, the individuals who were *extremely* ego-defensive did *not* respond well to this kind of influence attempt. The reason advanced was that for these people, the attitudes they held were so crucial to the maintenance of their personalities that some kind of psychiatric treatment would be a necessary forerunner of successful persuasion (Katz, Sarnoff & McClintock, 1956). *

Discussion

There is a valuable lesson in these experiments and in the reasoning of the researchers responsible for them. The findings show that

---

* This experiment, with some modifications, was repeated at another time with another group of subjects. The results were substantially the same as those already reported (Katz, McClintock & Sarnoff, 1957).

when the factors underlying attitudes are taken into account, persuasion is more likely to be successful. Successful persuasion depends on an understanding of why an audience should want to accept your point of view or buy your product.

Within the last two decades research on people's buying habits has undergone a considerable change. The change reflects an awareness on the part of advertising and marketing men of the need to know more about the personal factors underlying consumer brand preferences. This research emphasis has been named motivation research. * The justification for motivation research lies in the assumption that people often are attracted to or repelled by a particular brand of product for reasons that the purchaser himself may be unaware of, or unwilling to discuss with an interviewer.

Here is an illustration. Some clothing made from synthetic fibers is washable, and dries relatively free of wrinkles. It might be supposed that such "wash and wear" clothing would have immediate appeal to housewives as it requires little if any ironing before being worn. It is not very helpful for a manufacturer of such wash and wear garments to learn that some women refuse to buy them. But a consumer research study which attempts to discover the reasons underlying resistance to buying such clothing might reveal that (1) some women are still unaware of the no-ironing feature of the fabrics; (2) some women feel their neighbors might be critical of them for turning out a family in clothes that were not ironed; (3) some women might think they are not fulfilling their roles as housewives if they attempted to cut out any of the key household chores, such as ironing. These reasons correspond to the factual, social and personal bases for attitudes which were discussed earlier. Each of these reasons requires a somewhat different advertising and promotional effort. Women who do not yet know of the no-ironing feature may be persuaded to buy if the facts about the fabrics are presented to them. Women who fear the criticism of their neighbors might be persuaded by advertisements which show people like themselves enjoying the advantages of wash and wear clothing. And women who feel that to fulfill their roles as housewives requires a certain amount of ironing drudgery, might be persuaded by an

---

For an example of how one investigator describes the motivations underlying man's purchasing behavior see: Kotler, P. Behavioral models for analyzing buyers. *Journal of Marketing*, 1965, *29*, 37–45. Nondemographic analyses, "psychographics," psychological or attitudinal market segmentation are all concepts that have evolved out of the motivation research idea; all attempt to relate personal or social characteristics of consumers with their buying behavior.

insight approach: helping them understand why it is so important to them to play the part of housewife in such a particular and inflexible way. *

Suggested Readings: Motivations Underlying Attitudes

(1) Katz, D. The functional approach to the study of attitudes. *Public Opinion Quarterly,* 1960, *24,* 163-204.

(2) Katz, D., Sarnoff, I., & McClintock, C. Ego-defense and attitude change. *Human Relations,* 1956, *9,* 27-45.

(3) Kotler, P. Behavioral models for analyzing buyers. *Journal of Marketing,* 1965, *29,* 37-45.

---

* This example, though somewhat dated, has been retained in this edition for its illustrative value.

**The individual's personality traits affect his suscepti-
bility to persuasion.**

Thus far we have spent most of our time writing about persuasive
appeals without paying much attention to personality differences
among individuals exposed to those appeals. Some persuaders
choose to ignore personality differences altogether—thinking the
impact of their message will be the same on all their listeners regardless of any individual differences between them. Such reasoning, of course, is fallacious; there is ample evidence to indicate that
the same appeal is received and acted upon differently by different
listeners due to variations in their personality characteristics.
Three such characteristics—intelligence, authoritarianism and integrative complexity—are examined in this section.

During the past decade an increasing number of investigators
have become interested in exploring the relationship between personality traits and persuasibility—an interest kindled in large part
by publication of the Hovland and Janis *Personality and Persuasibility* volume in 1959. Today there are literally hundreds of studies
on the topic—enough information to fill several books. Obviously
we cannot do justice to the area in the space of a few pages; what
we will try to do is give the reader a feeling for the type of research
being conducted in this domain and also show how personality
does influence an individual's susceptibility to persuasion.

Intelligence and Persuasion

Specimen studies

1. In an experiment by Carment, Miles and Cervin (1965) 248
undergraduates were given a battery of tests designed to determine:
(1) intelligence; (2) introversion-extroversion (see Eysenck, 1957);
(3) opinions on several topics (e.g., the quality of products manufactured in America). From this initial sample of students a final
subject selection was made, based on individual responses to the
three tests. These remaining subjects were then divided into pairs
to discuss one of the opinion topics they had disagreed on. Subject
pairings pitted: (1) high intelligent-extroverted vs high intelligent-
extroverted; (2) high intelligent-extroverted vs high intelligent-

introverted; and (3) high intelligent-extroverted vs low intelligent-extroverted.

Subjects were judged on their *persuasiveness* and *persuasibility*. Persuasiveness was defined as: (1) the tendency to speak first and (2) speak the greatest amount during the discussion. Persuasibility was defined as the "tendency to change or not to change opinion when placed in a persuasion situation which requires arguing a topic with an individual who holds an opposing opinion."

Findings: Results indicate that the more intelligent and extroverted subjects are more persuasive (talk first and most) and less persuasible (change their opinion less frequently) in arguing their point of view with a disagreeing opponent (Carment, Miles & Cervin, 1965).

2. One experimenter had a group of high school students indicate how they felt about various national groups, religious sects, political parties, etc. Some time later the students were exposed to a communication containing crudely propagandistic statements about each of the groups they had rated. The intelligence of the group was estimated from their scores on a standard intelligence test.

Findings: The most intelligent students were the least influenced by this kind of propaganda (Wegrocki, 1934).

3. During World War II, many experiments were carried on to test the effectiveness of the *Why We Fight* films which were produced for troop indoctrination. Opinions on the subject of a film were ascertained by the use of a questionnaire, both before and after the showing. The measure of intelligence which the investigators used was years of schooling completed.

Findings: The films were in general more effective on the soldiers of higher intelligence. There were reversals in this trend, however, especially on opinion questions, but not so much for factual questions (Hovland, Janis & Kelley, 1953).

Discussion

An examination of data from the *Why We Fight* films led to the conclusion that an over-all score for general intelligence is made up of separate components, each of which helps to explain the experimental results: (1) learning ability—the brighter people learn and remember more; (2) critical ability—the brighter people can sort out the reasonable arguments from the specious ones; (3) inference-drawing ability—the brighter people can see the implications behind the facts.

From this kind of reasoning about intelligence and susceptibility to persuasion, two hypotheses were formulated (Hovland, Janis & Kelley, 1953):

(1) "Persons with high intelligence will tend—mainly because of their ability to draw valid inferences—to be *more* influenced than those with low intellectual ability when exposed to persuasive communications which rely primarily on impressive logical arguments."

(2) "Persons with high intelligence will tend—mainly because of their superior critical ability—to be *less* influenced than those with low intelligence when exposed to persuasive communications which rely primarily on unsupported generalities or false, illogical, irrelevant argumentation."

Suggested Readings: Intelligence and Persuasion

(1) Carment, D., Miles, C., & Cervin, V. Persuasiveness and persuasibility as related to intelligence and extraversion. *British Journal of Social and Clinical Psychology*, 1965, *4*, 1-7.

Authoritarianism and Persuasion

One kind of personality characteristic has been the basis for several experiments in attitude change. This is the so-called authoritarian personality (Adorno, et al., 1950). There are really a number of related traits that are characteristic of an authoritarian personality. One of them is a tendency to have unquestioned respect for people in authority, those with power, such as the parent has in the eyes of the child, the boss to some of his employees, the military leader, the business tycoon, etc. The availability of psychological tests that single out people with authoritarian personalities from other kinds of people has made it possible for researchers to identify these people for persuasion experiments.

Specimen studies

1. One experimenter reasoned that the authoritarian type of person could be swayed by an appeal from an authority, someone who

was known to be a powerful individual. Persons who are not themselves authoritarian in nature should be better swayed by an informational type of appeal, whereas just giving information to the authoritarian type of person should not have a marked effect on his attitudes.

The topic chosen for the experiment was attitudes toward blacks. Four groups of subjects were used, about 50 people in each group. At a first meeting all subjects completed a questionnaire which contained questions to ascertain their attitudes towards blacks and other questions that would classify them as authoritarian or non-authoritarian types. Each group met separately the second time and was exposed to a particular kind of communication:

Group 1: These people read an information booklet which presented facts about the changes in educational, health, and occupational position of blacks during the last century.

Group 2: This group was exposed to an authoritarian communication which was pro-black in nature. They were presented with comments about blacks that were attributed to business and military leaders. Here is an example of a comment supposedly made by a majority of business leaders: ". . . workers should be rewarded for productive effort . . . segregation and discrimination have prevented the full operation of rewards and promotions in the American incentive system."

Group 3: Like the previous group, these people were also given an authoritarian treatment, but one that was anti-Negro in nature. They too were exposed to some remarks supposedly made by business and military leaders. Example: "If the American economic system is not to be endangered, freedom to invest capital, to realize profits, and to enter or to refuse to enter into a contractual relationship with any group must be preserved at all costs. Thus, freedom to serve or to refuse service to Negroes is a matter to be decided entirely by the individual who is risking his capital in a business venture."

Group 4: This was a control group that filled out the before and after questionnaires but was not exposed to any communication in between.

At a third experimental session, each of the four groups once more filled out the questionnaire which measured their attitudes toward Negroes.

Findings: The people who had been identified as authoritarian were swayed by the remarks of the authority figures, regardless of whether the remarks were pro-Negro or anti-Negro. The non-authoritarian people were persuaded more by the information booklet than they were by the remarks of the authority figures. Lastly, the authoritarian subjects were influenced less by the information booklet than they were by the authority figures. All of the findings are in line with the predictions made before the experiment started (Rohrer & Sherif, 1951). *

Suggested Readings: Authoritarianism and Persuasion

(1) Rohrer, J., & Sherif, M (eds.). *Social Psychology at the Crossroads.* New York: Harper, 1951.
(2) Steiner, I., & Johnson, H. Authoritarianism and conformity. *Sociometry,* 1963, *26,* 21-34.

Integrative Complexity and Persuasion

Although most readers are quite familiar with the concepts of "intelligence" and "authoritarianism," fewer have probably heard of "integrative complexity." When we use this term we are referring to the way a person thinks—the method by which he seeks and utilizes information in his daily life. According to Conceptual Systems theory (Harvey, Hunt & Schroder, 1961; Schroder, Driver & Streufert, 1967) thinking ability varies among individuals (as does intelligence) and is measured in terms of its integrative complexity. A person high in integrative complexity is called "abstract." A person low in integrative complexity is labeled "concrete."

Theoretically and experimentally, there are many differences between the concrete and abstract individual. A concrete person is relatively rigid and closed minded in his thinking. His ability to utilize information in new and meaningful ways is limited; he is not a complex thinker. An abstract individual, on the other hand, is a flexible and original thinker. In a word, the person high in integrative complexity is "creative" (Karlins, 1967; Karlins & Lamm, 1967).

---

* More recent studies (Smith, 1965; Steiner & Johnson, 1963) caution against blanket consideration of the authoritarian as a conformist. Under some conditions he does not conform so readily.

From Conceptual Systems theory one can make predictions about how individuals varying in integrative complexity will behave in persuasive situations. Many such predictions have been tested in experimental situations. An example of one such experiment is presented as Specimen Study 1 below.

Specimen studies

1. Using a sensory deprivation condition (where subjects were required to remain silent in a darkened room for 23 hours) Suedfeld and Vernon (1966) set out to test two hypotheses derived from Conceptual Systems theory: abstract subjects (in comparison to concrete individuals) will: (1) be less easily swayed by a propaganda appeal; (2) have a greater need for information in their environment. 248 male college students took tests designed to measure their: (1) level of integrative complexity and (2) attitudes toward Turkey and the Turkish people. From this group 28 students were selected to participate in the experiment—based on their extreme scores on the complexity test and their expressed neutrality toward Turks. Subjects were tested in one of two experimental conditions: sensory deprivation group (7 abstract; 7 concrete) and a nonconfined control group (7 abstract; 7 concrete). In both experimental conditions, at the end of 23 hours, subjects were exposed to a two-sided propaganda statement on Turks. The first part of the communication was "Pro-Turk" ("Turkish justice is swift and impartial, as seen when . . .") followed by a negative segment ("On the other hand, the police force and the courts are sometimes overhasty and harsh; for example . . ."). After the presentation of the two-sided communication, subjects were asked three questions concerning their opinions about Turks (items from the attitude test they took earlier). If at least two of the subject's responses were "Pro-Turk" he was given a new two-sided communication; if, on the other hand, he gave less than two "Pro-Turk" answers, a ten minute silence followed, after which the first communication was repeated. All subjects understood, from the beginning of the experiment, that hearing new information about Turks was contingent on answering the majority of the opinion questions correctly. The "correct answer" was a "Pro-Turk" answer—a fact readily apparent to the subject. Thus, the individual who desired new information was forced to display compliant behavior: give "Pro-Turk" responses to the experimenter's questions. Of course, willingness to give "Pro-Turk" answers to gain information doesn't necessarily signify attitude

change toward Turks. To assess this factor, the Turk attitude scale was readministered to subjects at the completion of the experiment—when answers would not gain the subjects any "rewards."

> *Findings:* Integratively complex individuals—"whose need for information is relatively high and who find sensory deprivation more unpleasant than do concretes"—showed a higher degree of compliance in order to obtain information during sensory deprivation than integratively simple subjects (made more "Pro-Turk" responses to hear the two-sided communications). Yet, after sensory deprivation, abstract subjects showed *less* attitude change toward Turks than did concrete subjects (as reflected in scores on the post-experimental Turk attitude scale). Thus, both experimental hypotheses—that abstract subjects would seek more information but would be less vulnerable to persuasive appeals—were confirmed (Suedfeld & Vernon, 1966).

Discussion

In exploring the topic of personality and persuasion certain questions come up again and again. You may have asked one of them yourself—for instance, *whether susceptibility to persuasion may itself be a personality trait.* If such a trait did exist, it would be fascinating to study and vital to know about. When we speak of "susceptibility to persuasion as a personality trait" we are referring to a tendency by the individual to show consistency of response to persuasive appeals across a wide variety of situations. If such a trait were fact then we would expect a person high in susceptibility to persuasion to be easily swayed by persuasive appeals in many different contexts. For a person low in such susceptibility we would expect the opposite results.

Thus far scientists disagree on whether such a personality trait exists. Some support Harriet Linton and Elaine Graham (1959) who claim: ". . . persuasibility is not an isolated phenomenon, but is rather the product of certain underlying attributes of the personality. Personality patterns apparently make a person more or less susceptible to influence in a wide variety of situations, whether the influence arises from the structure of the external field, from another person, or from a written communication." Other investigators believe some people will be more influenced in one situation, other people in a different situation. Nobody will resist every persuasive appeal and nobody will be vulnerable to all of them. In other words, there is no general trait of susceptibility to persuasion.

The problem of individual consistency in persuasibility is further complicated by variables such as "involvement." When a person is deeply involved in an issue (e.g., a Vietnam infantryman hearing a persuasive appeal against air-fighter cover in Vietnam) it seems he responds differently than when he is uninvolved (e.g., the same soldier hearing a persuasive communication on the superiority of butter over margarine).* Thus, even if there were a personality trait of "susceptibility to persuasion" this response tendency might be overshadowed by the individual's involvement in a given issue (e.g., our Vietnam infantryman, if normally susceptible to persuasion, would probably not be swayed by the appeal aimed at removing protective aircraft from the front!).

Based on current evidence it seems safest to say that no general personality trait of susceptibility to persuasion has been clearly established. Rather, individuals with certain specified personality traits and needs are likely to be more readily persuaded by certain kinds of appeals.

"Why study the relationship between personality and persuasion at all?" is another frequent inquiry. Some readers may feel that of all the aspects of persuasion that could be examined, the least useful to the practicing persuader would be those that have to do with individual personality traits. If all shades of every trait are present in a mass audience, what good are personality data? There are several reasons why such data are valuable:

(1) In many instances the persuader will confront an audience that is highly selected, whose members may exhibit a preponderance of similar characteristics. Readers of the *Wall Street Journal*, for example, are often not the same kind of people as readers of the *Village Voice*. Furthermore, readers of each of these newspapers are likely to be similar to other readers of the same newspaper in many ways: in their interests, way of life, range of income, political affiliations, etc.

(2) As more becomes known about the influence of the small group on its members, communicators will devote more thought to how they can capitalize on similarities of personality and circumstance which bring people together in the same neighborhood, work

---

* See, for example, Eagly & Manis (1966), Miller (1965) and Sherif & Sherif (1967).

group, social club, and other centers of influence, e.g., readership of the *Wall Street Journal*.

(3) A continuing awareness of the existence and force of individual characteristics will help any persuader to avoid the trap of seeing his audience as a lump of humanity instead of as separate, distinct individuals.

Suggested Readings: Integrative Complexity

(1) Schroder, H., Driver, M., & Streufert, S. *Human information processing: Individuals and groups in complex social situations.* New York: Holt, 1967.

(2) Suedfeld, P., & Vernon, J. Attitude manipulation in restricted environments: II. Conceptual structure and the internalization of propaganda received as a reward for compliance. *Journal of Personality and Social Psychology,* 1966, *3,* 586-589.

6

THE PERSUADER

Does a man have to believe in the persuader before he believes in his message?

When is belief in the persuader less important in changing opinions?

Are there ways to enhance the persuasiveness of the low-credibility communicator?

Will a communicator be more persuasive if he agrees with his audience on some issue not directly related to his appeal?

Are people's opinions about a persuader affected by what he tells them?

Should a persuader try for a maximum of opinion change or just a little opinion change?

Is a persuasive appeal more readily accepted by listeners who share certain similarities with the communicator?

There will be more opinion change in the desired direction if the communicator has high credibility than if he has low credibility.

The topic of source credibility brings to mind a classroom demonstration popular in introductory psychology courses. At the beginning of class the professor introduces a "Dr. Hans Schmidt" to the students, informing them that the guest is a "research chemist of international renown currently employed by the U.S. Government to study the properties of gas diffusion." Dr. Schmidt, clad in a full length white lab coat and sporting a well-tended goatee, then steps forward and, in a heavy German accent, tells the class he wishes to test the properties of a new chemical vapor he has developed. Specifically," he says, "I wish to determine how quickly the vapor diffuses throughout the room and how readily people can detect it." Pointing to a small glass beaker the doctor continues: "Therefore I would ask your cooperation in a little experiment. I am going to pull this stopper and release the vapor. It is completely harmless but purposely treated to smell like gas—the kind you smell around a stove when the burner doesn't ignite. This particular sample is highly odorous so no one should have any trouble detecting its presence. What I want you to do is raise your hand as soon as you smell the vapor. Are there any questions?" At this point the "chemist" pulls the stopper and releases the "vapor." Very soon, and in a very orderly manner, hands begin going up—first in the front rows and then on back—like a wave rolling through the lecture hall. Obviously satisfied, the visiting scientist replaces the stopper, thanks the class for its cooperation, and leaves the room. Later on the professor informs his class that the "chemist" was in reality a faculty member from the German Department, and the "vapor" nothing more than distilled water.

Why, then, did nearly everyone smell gas? Wouldn't you have—considering the circumstances? After all, didn't a famous chemist say the gas would be odorous and readily detected? The power of suggestion. A suggestion made even more powerful by the *credibility* of the persuader making the suggestion.

Just what is source credibility? Actually, it can be any number of factors (operating independently or in combination) that influence audience perception of the communicator's believability.

In the case of our research chemist the factor of "prestige" accounted for the high credibility of the source. Generally, the more credible the communicator, the more persuasive his appeal.* In other words, persuaders low in credibility will have more difficulty influencing behavior than an individual enjoying higher credibility.

Just what are these "factors" that determine the level of a communicator's credibility? Some of them are relatively obvious (although different people call them by different names)—for example, "prestige," "expertise," "trustworthiness," "point of view" and "sex" of the communicator. Then there are some "not so obvious" factors, e.g., skin color of the persuader (Aronson & Golden, 1962). The important thing for the reader to remember about factors influencing source credibility is that they vary as a function of each specific persuasive situation: the issue at hand, the persuader in question, and the audience involved.**

Specimen studies

1. In a recent study of source credibility Zagona and Harter (1966) exposed 57 undergraduates to an identical communication discussing the effects of smoking on health. One third of the subjects were told the message was from the *Surgeon General's Report on Smoking and Health* (high credibility source); another third of the subjects were led to believe the passage originated in *Life Magazine* (moderate credibility source); the remaining 19 subjects were informed the communication was an advertisement by the American Tobacco Company (low credibility source).

After reading the passage on smoking all subjects were given an 18-item test designed to see how well they remembered the message and their attitudes toward it.

> *Findings:* (1) the communication was better remembered when it was attributed to low and high (rather than medium) credibility sources; (2) "As credibility of the source increased, the percentage of subjects who agreed with the information

---

* One possible exception to this "rule" has been pointed out by cognitive dissonance theorists who claim that sometimes the negative (low-credibility) communicator can be more persuasive (Brehm & Cohen, 1962; Festinger, 1957; Zimbardo, Weisenberg, Firestone & Levy, 1965).

** Rosnow and Robinson (1967) make an important point on this subject, stating that "whether or not a communicator is credible depends on the point of view of the recipient of his communication. To paraphrase an old saying, *credibility is in the eye of the beholder.*"

and perceived it as trustworthy also increased" (Zagona & Harter, 1966).

2. Two groups of college students were exposed to identical communications on problematical aspects of antihistamine drugs, atomic submarines, the steel shortage, and the future of movie theaters. In half the cases the stated source of the argument was a person who had high credibility with the students, and in the other cases the communicator was a person of low credibility. The communicators identified with the arguments had been previously rated by the students to establish how much weight they carried. Questionnaires administered before and after the communications were the basis for estimating opinon change.

> *Findings:* In most instances, opinion change in the direction advocated by the persuader was much greater when the persuader had high credibility than when he had low credibility (Hovland & Weiss, 1951).

3. In another study of persuader credibility a speech advocating lenient treatment of juvenile delinquents was heard by groups of high school students. The students were told that the speech was a radio program for them to evaluate. Three different introductions to the same speech were tape-recorded for use on different groups. In one introduction the speaker was identified as a judge in juvenile court. In another introduction (to get a neutral source) the speaker was established as just someone picked out of the studio audience. In a third introduction the speaker was also made out to be from the studio audience, but as the announcer interviewed him, it developed that the speaker had a criminal record and had himself been a juvenile delinquent. In the course of the post-experimental questionnaire, the students were asked to rate the speaker on the fairness and impartiality of his remarks.

> *Findings:* The "judge" was rated as having given a fair presentation more than twice as many times as the "ex-criminal." There was significantly more of the desired opinion change from the students who heard the "judge" than from the stu-

dents who heard the "ex-criminal" (Kelman & Hovland, 1953).*

Discussion

Every day we judge speakers on the basis of their "credibility," and often our decision to accept or reject a persuasive appeal is directly contingent on such judgments. Most people would agree that physicians are more capable of diagnosing illness than most laymen; if you feel you need medical advice, you will undoubtedly accept your doctor's diagnosis over the opinion of a friend. On the other hand, we often run across "credibility by association," for instance, when a well-known athlete or movie star appears on the back cover of a magazine advising us to switch to his brand of after-shave lotion. Advertisers apparently think that credibility in one field can sometimes be exploited for its credibility value in another field (aside from the attention-getting value of a familiar face and name).

Here are two of the hypotheses which have been advanced to explain why credibility of source seems to affect opinion change:

(1) Whenever an audience decides that a communicator is untrustworthy, they pay less attention to him, and so expose themselves less to his message.

(2) Audiences have less motivation to accept what they read or hear when they have decided that the communicator is unreliable (Hovland, Janis & Kelley, 1953).

In recent years, since the first edition of this book, observers have talked about a "credibility gap" in our national government, an erosion of confidence in the credibility of administration spokesmen. Part of this condition may be attributed to the way that a particular administration chooses to manage the news, to select what it wants the public to know. But part of the problem lies also in the increasing demand on the public to take sides on issues which it is completely incompetent to evaluate, such as whether the country should deploy an anti-ballistic missile system, or whether television programming has too much violence.

---

* For other examples of how source credibility effects opinion change see: Kelman & Eagly (1965), Sargent & Webb (1966), Weiss (1967) and Whittaker & Meade (1968).

Suggested Readings: Source Credibility

(1) Weiss, R. Consensus technique for the variation of source credibility. *Psychological Reports,* 1967, *20,* 1159-1162.

(2) Zagona, S., & Harter, M. Credibility of source and recipient's attitude: Factors in the perception and retention of information on smoking behavior. *Perceptual and Motor Skills,* 1966, *23,* 155-168.

(3) Zimbardo, P., Weisenberg, M., Firestone, I., & Levy, B. Communicator effectiveness in producing public conformity and private attitude change. *Journal of Personality,* 1965, *33,* 233-255.

Credibility of the persuader may be less of a factor in opinion change later on than immediately after exposure.

The results of the two experiments described in Specimen Studies 2 and 3 on pages 110-111 reveal that more of the desired opinion change takes place when the persuasive message is ascribed to a highly credible source than when the message is attributed to someone of low credibility. The extent of opinion change was measured by questionnaires administered before and immediately after the influence attempt.

The experimenters also wanted to know if the credibility of the persuader was just as important after a lapse of time as it seemed to be immediately after the message was presented. Their hypothesis was that the effect of source credibility on opinion change becomes modified as time goes by. The same people who were subjects for the original experiments took part in extensions of them. The experimenters devised new forms of the previously administered attitude questionnaires. One group of subjects filled out these new questionnaires four weeks after they had been exposed to the persuasive message. In the case of the other group the time lapse was three weeks. The experimenters tested their hypothesis by comparing the questionnaires administered three and four weeks after exposure with the questionnaires administered immediately following exposure.

Findings: The effect of the persuader's credibility did tend to wear off with time. For example, the people who had been exposed to the low credibility sources showed *more* of an opinion change in the desired direction after a lapse of time than they showed immediately following exposure. (This is another case of the "sleeper effect" discussed earlier.) Also, the people who had been exposed to the high credibility sources showed *less* of the desired opinion change after a lapse of time than was evident right after exposure. The net effect was that all the subjects showed about the same amount of opinion change after three or four weeks. The effects of source credibility tended to wash out with time (Hovland & Weiss, 1951; Kelman & Hovland, 1953).

Discussion

More than one publicity-wise gentleman has been credited with the quote, "I don't care what you print about me in the newspapers, as long as you spell my name right." Behind this bit of public relations folklore lies a kind of reasoning that is related to the preceding findings—that as time passes there is a separation in the reader's or listener's mind between what was said and who said it. To put it another way, the findings seem to suggest that a high credibility source may be important if the persuasion attempt is designed to get immediate results (signing a petition, taking a vote, etc.). However, if the aim of persuasion is long term, then the believability of the communicator may not be such a crucial issue.

Suggested Readings: Source Credibility "Sleeper Effect"

(1) Hovland, C., & Weiss, W. The influence of source credibility on communication effectiveness. *Public Opinion Quarterly,* 1951, *15,* 635-650.

The persuasiveness of a low-credibility communicator can be enhanced when he argues against his own best interest or when he is identified after, rather than before, presentation of his appeal.

It stands to reason that not every persuader can be perceived as highly credible. To assume otherwise is certainly a heady case of over-optimism! What then of the low credibility communicator? Is there some way he can be persuasive? We should hope so; otherwise the authors might never win an argument with their wives. Fortunately, recent studies have suggested ways to increase the persuasiveness of the low credibility communicator.

Specimen studies

1. Can a criminal (low credibility source) be more persuasive than a prosecuting attorney (high credibility source)? This was the question investigated by Walster, Aronson and Abrahams in two experiments published in 1966.* The same hypothesis, tested in both studies, predicted ". . . a communicator, regardless of his general prestige, will be more effective and will be seen as more credible when arguing for a position opposed to his own best interest, than when arguing for changes obviously in his own interest."

To test their assumption, the experimenters first gave high school students an attitude questionnaire designed to assess their opinions on the topic: "How much power should Portuguese prosecutors and police possess in dealing with criminals?" Then subjects were exposed to one of four persuasive communications: (1) a low credibility source (criminal) arguing against his own best interest (Portuguese prosecutors should have *more* power); (2) a low credibility source (criminal) arguing in favor of his own best interest (Portuguese prosecutors should have *less* power); (3) a high credibility source (prosecutor) arguing against his own best interest (Portuguese prosecutors should have *less* power); (4) a high credibility source (prosecutor) arguing in favor of his own best interest (Portuguese prosecutors should have *more* power). Finally, after reading the persuasive appeals, subjects' attitudes on the issue

---

* Because of the similarities between the two experiments (procedures and results), we will limit our discussion to the second investigation.

of power for prosecutors were reassessed, along with their opinions on how credible the communicator seemed to be.

> *Findings:* The hypothesis was supported. "When the prosecutor advocated less power for prosecutors, he was much more effective than was a criminal advocating the same position. However, when the criminal insisted that prosecutors should have more power, he was much more effective than a prosecutor advocating the same position." Further, the persuader (whether criminal or prosecutor) was judged more credible when arguing against his own best interests. The authors conclude: "When arguing against his own self-interest, a communicator who would normally be considered to have low prestige can be extremely effective—in fact, even more effective than a high prestige communicator presenting the same argument" (Walster, Aronson & Abrahams, 1966).

2. General Westmoreland is a "hawk" on the Vietnam war. Assume you have two statements supposedly voiced by the general. One comment is congruous with his previous attitudes on the conflict: "U.S. bombing of North Vietnam has partially reduced the influx of men and military supplies to the South." The other statement is incongruous with the general's previous position: "Generally speaking, the number of U.S. casualties in the Vietnam conflict has far exceeded that reported in the U.S. press." Assume further you have two statements attributed to black activist Stokely Carmichael—once again, one congruent ("There are many documented reports of extensive police brutality in Negro neighborhoods") and the other incongruent ("Often Negroes have not taken the initiative required to benefit from civil rights legislation"). Now imagine that you present the Westmoreland and Carmichael statements to subjects in an experiment in the following manner: every individual is exposed to one statement (congruous or incongruous) made by Westmoreland and Carmichael; sometimes these subjects are told who made the comments, sometimes not. In such a situation which statements will be judged most credible, the communications consistent with or opposed to the known ideological positions of Westmoreland and Carmichael?

This question—asked by Drs. Koeske and Crano in a 1968 study— is similar to the one posed by Walster, Aronson and Abrahams in Specimen Study 1 on p. 115. Both inquiries are concerned with the possible enhancement of communicator persuasiveness through in-

creasing the credibility of his appeal; and both are examined by
having a communicator make a statement opposed to his own best
interests (in one case criminals and prosecutors making incongruous comments about the power of the court; in the other a military officer and black activist making incongruous remarks about
Vietnam and the black community). Were the Koeske and Crano
findings consistent with those of Walster, Aronson and Abrahams?

> *Findings:* In a most important respect, yes. Once again a
> statement was judged more credible when it was voiced by a
> communicator arguing against his own best interests. Thus,
> for example, the statment "Generally speaking, the number of
> U.S. casualties in the Vietnamese conflict has far exceeded
> that reported in the U.S. press" was judged more credible
> when attributed to Westmoreland than when presented
> anonymously (Koeske & Crano, 1968).*

Thus far we have examined two studies which suggest one way
a low credibility communicator can become more persuasive—
namely, by making statements inconsistent with his own best interests. Such communications are viewed by audiences as being
more credible; and, generally, the more credible the communication, the more persuasive the communicator.

But what of the low credibility communicator who doesn't wish
to make statements against his previously established convictions?
Is there no hope for this individual as a persuader?

3. A study by Greenberg and Miller (1966) offers yet another way
of reducing the low credibility communicator problem in persuasive appeals. These investigators predict that: "When the source
has low credibility, attribution of the message to the source after
presentation of the message will result in more favorable audience
attitudes toward the proposal than when the message is attributed
to the source prior to presentation of the message." In other words,
to reduce the negative impact of a low credibility communicator,
identify him *after* he has presented his message! The reasoning
behind this hypothesis is relatively straightforward. If a listener
knows in advance of a communication that the speaker may be

---

* This finding was not a direct effect of source credibility. The statement
about the effectiveness of bombing North Vietnam (congruous with Westmoreland) was judged about equally credible whether authored by Westmoreland or
given anonymously.

unreliable or untrustworthy, he may ignore the message completely ("tune out") —discounting the information as worthless. On the other hand, if the listener finds out about the qualifications of the speaker after hearing the communication there will be a greater likelihood that he at least paid attention to the message and will be swayed by some of the arguments (irrespective of the communicator's credibility).

Greenberg and Miller tested their hypothesis in a series of experiments. In one of the investigations two groups of undergraduates were exposed to the same message detailing the possible hazards of constant toothbrushing. One group was informed, *before they read the passage,* that a low credibility source had composed it; the second group was told about the source *after they read the material.* Once all subjects had read the communication, they filled out a survey designed to assess their attitudes toward the message topic (e.g., "Brushing one's teeth can become a harmful practice, if one does it too often.").

> *Findings:* The most favorable attitudes toward the message topic were expressed by the subjects who were informed of the low credibility of the communicator *after* they had read the persuasive appeal. Summarizing their series of experiments, Greenberg and Miller conclude: "The most provocative result of the present studies is the thrice-replicated finding that the effects of low credibility can be largely obviated by delaying source identification until after a message has been presented. In each experiment in which time of identification was manipulated, delayed identification of the low credible source enhanced the persuasiveness of the message" (Greenberg & Miller, 1966). *

Suggested Readings: Increasing Low Credibility Communicator Effectiveness

(1) Greenberg, B., & Miller, G. The effects of low-credible sources on message acceptance. *Speech Monographs,* 1966, *33,* 127-136.

(2) Koeske, G., & Crano, W. The effect of congruous and incongruous source-statement combinations upon the judged credi-

---

* Support for the Greenberg and Miller hypothesis also comes from Husek (1965).

bility of a communication. *Journal of Experimental Social Psychology*, 1968, *4*, 384-399.

(3) Walster, E., Aronson, E., & Abrahams, D. On increasing the persuasiveness of a low prestige communicator. *Journal of Experimental Social Psychology*, 1966, *2*, 325-342.

A communicator's effectiveness is increased if he initially expresses some views that are also held by his audience.

Frequently a persuasive speech or article includes opinions on more than one topic. Some propagandists have felt that an audience can be made to accept their point of view on a particular topic more easily, if, along with the discussion of the topic, they express other opinions which are known to agree with what the audience believes. For example, a speaker whose purpose is to convince a veterans' group of the need for high tariffs might begin his talk with some remarks favoring a veterans' bonus. One author has labeled this device "flogging the dead horse" (Weiss, 1957).

Specimen studies

1. An experiment was conducted to see if "flogging the dead horse" adds to the effectiveness of a persuasive communication. A questionnaire asking for opinions on a variety of topics was administered to 120 college students. The students also indicated how strongly they felt about each of their expressed opinions. Based on the responses to the questionnaire, the experimenter chose an issue on which to build a persuasive communication, and an issue that was to be used as the "dead horse." The topic of fluoridation of drinking water was chosen for the persuasive communication because most of the students were pro-fluoridation, but did not feel strongly about it. The persuasive communication was intended to win them over to an anti-fluoridation point of view. The topic of academic freedom was a natural choice to be the dead horse because students were almost unanimously in favor of it, and felt strongly about it. The dead horse communication was, of course, presented to agree with the students' viewpoint, favorable to the concept of academic freedom.

For purposes of the experiment, some students were presented with the communication on academic freedom followed by the communication on fluoridation. Other students were exposed to a neutral communication followed by the communication on fluoridation. As a last step in the experiment, all groups filled out the opinion questionnaire again.

Findings: The group that received the dead horse treatment
were won over to the desired viewpoint on the fluoridation
issue more than the groups that did not get the treatment
(Weiss, 1957).

Discussion

The author of the dead horse experiment suggests why the technique may be effective. The act of establishing agreement with an
audience on one issue puts a damper on their critical capacities
during the presentation of the next issue. The author carefully
points out, however, that the actual persuasive argument still has to
be a good one. It will not automatically be accepted just because
a dead horse issue was presented first. But there will be less resistance to accepting it.

Suggested Readings: "Beating the Dead Horse"

(1) Weiss, W. Opinion congruence with a negative source on one
    issue as a factor influencing agreement on another issue.
    Journal of Abnormal and Social Psychology, 1957, *54,* 180-
    186.

What an audience thinks of a persuader may be directly influenced by what they think of his message.

A possible by-product of exposing an audience to a persuasive communication is that they will change their opinion of the persuader in addition to, or maybe instead of, being influenced by his argument.

Specimen studies

1. In a series of experiments conducted at four universities in Japan, Elliot McGinnies wondered if audience impressions of a speaker would "vary as a function of the position taken by the speaker on a political issue." To find out he exposed 364 students to one of the following tape-recorded persuasive appeals: (1) a pro-American communication on the cold war; (2) a pro-Soviet communication on the cold war; (3) a pro-American communication on the Cuban missile crisis; (4) a pro-Soviet communication on the Cuban missile crisis; (5) a communication favoring American submarine visits to Japanese ports; (6) a communication presenting arguments both for and against such visitations. Unknown to the subjects, the *same speaker* was utilized to present the various communications (the same communicator, for example, presented both the pro-American and pro-Soviet messages on the cold war). Thus, any differences in listener perceptions of the communicator should have been a function of what he said, not how he said it.

Immediately after hearing the persuasive communications, subjects filled out a survey designed to assess their opinions of the speaker. Part of the survey contained pairs of bi-polar adjectives: "uninformed-informed," "dishonest-honest," "unintelligent-intelligent" (plus six others). Subjects were asked to "check the one adjective in each pair that applied most aptly to the speaker."

> *Findings:* What the listener thought of the persuader was directly influenced by the contents of his communication. For example, one sample of female subjects perceived the speaker, in the role of U.S. defender on the cold war issue, as significantly "more honest, sincere, interesting, strong, informed, and intelligent" than when reading the pro-Soviet argument (McGinnies, 1968).

2. One researcher started with two related hypotheses about the connection between the audience's opinion of the persuader and opinion of his message: (1) the more favorable the opinion the audience has of the persuader, the more likely it is to be influenced by his message; (2) the more an audience is already in agreement with a message, the more likely that its opinion of the persuader will go up; and the more it is already in disagreement with the message, the more likely that its opinion of the persuader will go down. Three sources of communication and three topics were paired for the experiment:

Source	*Topic*
Labor Leaders	Legalized Gambling
Chicago Tribune	Accelerated College Programs
Senator Robert Taft	Abstract Art

These sources and topics were selected on the basis of pretest results which showed that approximately the same number of subjects had favorable, unfavorable, and neutral attitudes toward each source and each topic. Two versions of each set of materials were made: in one version the source said something favorable about the topic; in the other version the source said something unfavorable about the topic. Some neutral stories were also prepared.

During the first of two sessions, each group that took part in the experiment (over 400 people altogether) made separate ratings of their attitudes towards each source and each topic. At the second session, five weeks later, each group read the communication material, which was made up to look like regular newspaper stories. There were several forms of the communications. For example, one form might have contained a story that labor leaders had taken a favorable stand toward legalized gambling, that the *Chicago Tribune* had an editorial criticizing abstract art, and that Senator Taft had said something neither favorable nor unfavorable about accelerated college programs. In this way, favorable, unfavorable, and neutral statements by each source were rotated. Just after they had read the communications, the students were asked to write the essence of each story in 25 words or less. They also filled out attitude scales once again on each source and each topic.

Findings: The hypotheses were confirmed. The results showed, for example, that if a person who originally favored legalized gambling read a story which showed that labor leaders also favored legalized gambling, his attitude toward labor leaders became more favorable. Also found to be true: a person with negative feelings about labor leaders would be less inclined to favor something that labor leaders endorsed (Tannenbaum, 1956).

3. Another experiment also demonstrates that persuader and message are interrelated and that in the course of an influence attempt, audience attitudes toward both the persuader and the message may be changed. The experimenters started with three hypotheses about the effects of a news commentator on his audience: (1) the factual material that a commentator presents increases his audience's knowledge of those particular areas of information; (2) a commentator's prediction will influence his audience to have the same opinion that he expresses; (3) the people who change their opinions to agree with the commentator's prediction will have a more favorable attitude toward the commentator than people who were not exposed to his predictions.

A 15-minute Drew Pearson broadcast was recorded. A questionnaire was constructed on the basis of the material in the broadcast. One part of the questionnaire was a quiz on the factual sections of the broadcast. The second part was a group of opinion questions related to the predictions that Pearson made. In addition, some other questions were prepared to measure attitudes toward Pearson as a commentator.

The 145 college students who took part were divided into experimental and control groups. None of the students had heard the broadcast before. At the first meeting, both groups were administered the fact and opinion questionnaire based on the broadcast. A week later the experimental group heard the recording of the broadcast; the control group did not hear it. Then both groups were readministered the questionnaire they had filled out a week before, and also the questionnaire measuring their attitudes toward Pearson as a commentator.

Findings: The results of the first questionnaire showed that the experimental and control groups gave about the same answers to the factual and opinion questions based on the broadcast. As a result of hearing the broadcast, the experimental group knew much more than the control group did about the factual information. Also, the experimental group showed a marked change in their opinions in the direction of the predictions that Pearson made. Finally, and most important to this discussion, although neither the experimental nor the control group thought too highly of Drew Pearson, the experimental group showed more favorable attitudes toward him than did the control group which was not exposed to his broadcast (Freeman, Weeks, Ashley & Wertheimer, 1955).

Suggested Readings: Perception of the Communicator

(1) McGinnies, E. Studies in persuasion: V. Perceptions of a speaker as related to communication content. *Journal of Social Psychology,* 1968, *75,* 21-33.

(2) Tannenbaum, P. Initial attitude toward source and concept as factors in attitude change through communication. *Public Opinion Quarterly,* 1956, *20,* 413-426.

The more extreme the opinion change that the high credibility communicator asks for, the more actual change he is likely to get.

Just how much opinion change should the communicator demand of his audience? The persuader has good reason to wonder: his effectiveness is reduced if, on the one hand, he asks for less than he could have achieved; or, on the other, he asks for too much and alienates the listener altogether.* Psychologists have debated this question with unusual vigor due, in large measure, to opposing viewpoints held by "cognitive dissonance" and "social judgment" theorists. Although the issue is still open to debate, preliminary evidence does seem to support this principle: the more opinion change requested, the more achieved. **

Specimen studies

1. Fifty-one high school seniors were asked to fill out a twelve-item questionnaire. Each item was on a different topic, and was presented in the form of a statement to which the student reacted by indicating the extent of his agreement or disagreement, from "strongly agree" to "strongly disagree." One statement, for example, was, "All things considered, Washington was a greater president than Lincoln." For each statement, the student also picked from a list the authority whose opinion about the statement he would most respect. In the case of the statement about Washington and Lincoln, the authorities that the students had to pick from were teachers, historians, or parents.

A month later, the same questionnaire was administered again. The persuasion attempt was incorporated into the questionnaire

---

* Some experimenters (Bergin, 1962; Aronson, Turner & Carlsmith, 1963) have data which indicate that when the *low* credibility communicator asks for extreme opinion change he is *less* successful than when he requests more moderate change.

** Some investigators (e.g., Freedman, 1964; Whittaker, 1965) argue that this principle doesn't hold under conditions of high subject involvement (where ego-involving issues are concerned). They agree that under low involvement the more opinion change asked for, the more will be obtained. However, under high involvement more moderate demands will be necessary to get the desired change. These ideas are based in large part on the social judgement theory of Sherif and his colleagues (see: Hovland, Harvey & Sherif, 1957; Sherif & Hovland, 1961; Sherif & Sherif, 1967; Sherif, Sherif & Nebergall, 1965).

itself. That is, the students found a mark in one of the answer boxes beside each question. The mark showed how the question had been answered by the authorities for whom the students had indicated high respect when they filled out the same questionnaire a month earlier. For instance, if a student had chosen "historians" as the most respected source of the statement about Washington and Lincoln, then he was informed that the marked answer box beside that question reflected the views of historians.

This second questionnaire had been prepared individually for each subject based on his answers to the first questionnaire. For some questions, the opinion of the authority group was made to be very close to the opinion that the student had himself expressed the first time he filled out the questionnaire. For other questions, the authority group's opinions were made to be further apart from the student's opinions, sometimes much further apart. In this way, the experimenters were able to produce three degrees of discrepancy (slight, moderate, and marked) between the student's original opinions and the authority opinions.

Findings: A greater overall change in opinion in the expected direction was produced by a large discrepancy than by a small discrepancy between the students' opinions and the opinions of the authority groups. Or, in more general terms, communications that advocate a greater amount of change from an audience's view do in fact produce a greater amount of change than communications that advocate a position that is not much different from the position that the audience already holds (Hovland & Pritzker, 1957).

Suggested Readings: Amount of Opinion Change Requested

(1) Hovland, C., & Pritzker, H. Extent of opinion change as a function of amount of change advocated. *Journal of Abnormal and Social Psychology,* 1957, *54,* 257-261.

People are more persuaded by a communicator they perceive to be similar to themselves.

On page 120 we stated that "A communicator's effectiveness is increased if he initially expresses some views that are also held by his audience." In the context of the present discussion this should come as no surprise; after all, a persuader who agrees with the views of his audience is calling attention to his *similarities* with them on these issues. Think of your everyday behavior: wouldn't you be more likely to listen to, and agree with, someone with whom you had something in common? Of course, certain similarities between communicator and listener are more important than others in increasing persuasive impact. Researchers are currently trying to determine just what these "more important" similarities are. As the studies below will indicate, sometimes similarities need not be attitude congruencies between listener and persuader, but rather seemingly less "relevant" common characteristics like skin color uniformity between the communicator and his audience.

Specimen studies

1. Many investigators have felt that communicators are more effective when they are "liked" by their listeners (e.g., Brewer, 1968). In this context "liking" is viewed as a listener-perceived (and valued) similarity between himself and the persuader, brought about through the action (s) of the communicator. In a study of liking by Wright (1966) male undergraduates were first asked to complete a questionnaire designed to measure their opinions on the value of intercollegiate athletics. They were then assigned to a "group condition" where the topic of intercollegiate athletics was discussed by members communicating with each other by means of written notes. Unknown to subjects, the group interaction was regulated by the investigator so that one member—a confederate of the experimenter—initiated and controlled the flow of discussion. It was the task of this confederate to first get the subjects to like or dislike him and then to try to persuade them to lessen their favorable attitudes toward athletics. To create "either positive or negative relationships" between the confederate and the proper subjects, two friendly and two unfriendly "practice notes" (penned by the confederate to subjects before the actual "discussion" began) were sent out. The subject assigned to receive the friendly notes was sent these two pieces of correspondence:

> (1) "I'd sure like to get acquainted with you at least a little before we start the game, but I guess that's impossible with this screwy communication set-up. You'd probably like to know a little about me, too, even if we can't chat right now."
> (2) "Well, we got through one round okay. I'm kind of anxious to get started. I'm glad I can communicate directly to you; you seem like a good guy to talk to (even if it does have to be one-sided) ."

The subject chosen to get the unfriendly notes received the following information:

> (1) "I don't like the idea of conversing with virtual strangers, so I really have nothing to say to you. This note is just for the sake of practice, and doesn't mean I really want to communicate to you."
> (2) "I want to communicate to the guy in charge, and I guess the easiest way is to tell you to write a note to him. Write this message—and please be sure to get it right—'Person B thinks we've had enough practice to do an adequate job.' Be careful of the spelling and punctuation, too."

As might be suspected, the notes were successful in getting subjects to like or dislike the experimenter's confederate. Once these relationships were established, the confederate proceeded with his persuasion attempt: written messages designed to lower the opinions of subjects toward intercollegiate athletics. At the end of the "group discussion" all subjects were readministered the questionnaire on athletics.

> *Findings:* The experimenter's confederate was most persuasive when the subject liked rather than disliked him. In discussing persuasive appeals, the author notes: ". . . make sure the person you are trying to persuade likes you in the first place, or your efforts are likely to be in vain" (Wright, 1966) . *

---

* Similar findings were reported by Abelson and Miller (1967), who found subjects resisted persuasive appeals when the communicator insulted them.

2. A study by Mills and Jellison (1968) demonstrates just how pervasive and influential perceived similarities between listener and persuader can be in effecting opinion change. They asked four groups of college students to read an identical speech arguing that "every college student should receive a broad, general education." One group was told that a musician delivered the speech to music students; a second group that an engineer delivered the speech to engineering students; a third group that a musician delivered the speech to engineering students; and a fourth group that an engineer delivered the speech to music students. The experimenters hypothesized that "a communicator will be more persuasive when the audience thinks he feels similar to the audience he addresses than when the audience thinks the communicator feels dissimilar to those he addresses." Here, then, is a hypothesized case of the similarity principle operating in a "once removed" fashion: one group of listeners being differentially persuaded by a communicator on the basis of his supposed similarity or dissimilarity to a second group of listeners.

> *Findings:* The subjects who thought the persuader had presented his speech to a "similar" audience (musician speaking to musical students; or engineer speaking to engineering students) were more swayed by his communication than those thinking he had spoken to a "dissimilar" audience (musician speaking to engineering students; or engineer speaking to music students). Thus, the experimental hypothesis was supported (Mills & Jellison, 1968).

3. Sometimes "similarities" between a communicator and his audience that increase his persuasive impact have nothing to do with his message or personal attitudes. One such similarity is examined by Elliot Aronson and Burton Golden in their 1962 study of the persuasiveness of white vs black communicators on white elementary school children. In this investigation subjects were first asked (through questionnaires) their opinions on two topics: arithmetic and Negroes. Later the subjects were split into four groups and exposed to a speech "extolling the value and importance of arithmetic." Although the speech was identical for all four groups, the communicator giving it was not. Group 1 had a white speaker introduced as an engineer; Group 2 had a Negro speaker also introduced as an engineer; Group 3 had a white speaker introduced as a dishwasher; and Group 4 had a Negro speaker introduced as a dishwasher. Immediately after hearing the persuasive communication

all subjects again filled out a questionnaire tapping their opinions
on arithmetic. Of experimental interest: which communicator(s)
was most successful in getting his audience to value arithmetic?

> *Findings:* When the responses of all subjects were considered
> together it was found that the Negro engineer and white engi-
> neer were equally persuasive. "Moreover, both the Negro
> engineer and the white engineer were significantly more effec-
> tive than the Negro dishwasher, while neither was signif-
> icantly more effective than the white dishwasher. The white
> dishwasher was substantially more effective than the Negro
> dishwasher . . ." When subjects were divided into "preju-
> diced" and "unprejudiced" groups (based on their question-
> naire responses) the impact of skin color on opinion change
> was in far greater evidence. In this analysis, "not only was
> there a tendency for prejudiced individuals to be undersus-
> ceptible to the influence of a Negro communicator, but there
> was also a tendency for unprejudiced subjects to be over-
> susceptible to the influence of a Negro communicator." All
> in all, it is fair to say that perceived similarity between com-
> municator and listener on the basis of skin color is a factor in
> determining the ultimate impact of a persuasive appeal
> (Aronson & Golden, 1962). *

Discussion

We have seen that a communicator will be more persuasive if he
shares certain similarities with his audience.** Some of these similarities need not have anything to do with the communicator's message or attitudes on a specified topic. How many of us have rejected
a persuader's advice because we felt dissimilar to him? Probably
more than would care to admit. It seems safe to say that the most
persuasive communicator is probably one cast in our own image!

Suggested Readings: Communicator-Listener Similarities

(1) Aronson, E., & Golden, B. The effect of relevant and irrelevant
     aspects of communicator credibility on opinion change.
     Journal of Personality, 1962, *30,* 135-146.

---

* It is interesting to consider, in this respect, Bryan and Test's (1967) finding that white solicitors were superior to Negro solicitors in encouraging donors
to contribute to Salvation Army kettles.
** For additional studies on this topic see Berscheid, 1966; Brock, 1965; and
McGuckin, 1967.

(2) Mills, J., & Jellison, J. Effect on opinion change of similarity between the communicator and the audience he addresses. *Journal of Personality and Social Psychology*, 1968, *9*, 153-156.

(3) Wright, P. Attitude change under direct and indirect interpersonal influence. *Human Relations*, 1966, *19*, 199-211.

7

SOME CONCLUDING OBSERVATIONS ON PERSUASION

Brainwashing, subliminal advertising, truth serums, hypnosis: Do such forms of persuasion really work?

Are any scientists investigating ways to resist persuasion?

What are the implications of persuasion research for society?

Often the most "sensational" forms of persuasion are among the least effective in producing long-term attitude change.

If you ask the man on the street to tell you what he knows about scientific advances in the area of persuasion he will not give you a rundown of the psychological studies reported in the preceding chapters of this book. If he answers at all, he'll speak of brainwashing, hypnosis and other forms of supposed behavior control which have been popularized and sensationalized in the mass media. No wonder! It takes very little prodding to get someone interested in the topic of, say, mind-controlling drugs. The subject matter is very appealing, and the implications are awesome and immediate for John Q. Public. Consider, on the other hand, a documented presentation of the primacy-recency controversy in persuasion. Many willing or excited listeners here? We doubt it. Such a state of affairs is unfortunate; it has tended to focus public attention on areas of behavior control which (at least currently) are not highly effective persuasive devices and which, further, cast a sinister image over the entire field of persuasion (which is not sold on such techniques!). A noteworthy thing about such "extreme" forms of persuasion is they are often *less* effective in bringing about long-term attitude change than the less talked about, less "extreme" forms of manipulation outlined in the earlier sections of this volume!

Consider, for example, brainwashing. More than any other form of persuasion, brainwashing has stimulated the American imagination. Public interest in this topic grew out of the Korean War when American servicemen were exposed to brainwashing tactics on a grand scale for the first time, and such interest continues with every new movie and story on the topic. In reality, brainwashing is neither very new nor very effective. This was pointed out by Edgar Schein in a now classic study conducted on repatriated American servicemen in 1956. Based on personal interviews with liberated prisoners of war, Schein formulated a composite picture of brainwashing procedures in North Korean prison camps. His findings—that ". . . there is nothing new or terrifying about the specific (brainwashing) techniques used by the Chinese; they invented no mysterious devices for dealing with people"—remain valid today. It is true, as Schein also points out, that the Chinese did show some originality in combining several "traditional" devices (e.g., group discussion, self-criticism, interrogation, reward and punishment, forced confessions, propaganda and information control) into an overall persuasion blueprint for mind control. Yet for all their efforts only 21 prisoners out of thousands refused repatriation when it was offered.

James Brown, in his book *Techniques of Persuasion,* summarizes the impact of the Chinese efforts this way: "The significant point is that neither political indoctrination nor brainwashing showed any permanent results of the type intended, except in those cases who might have been expected to accept the beliefs engendered even if they had been offered them under normal circumstances. Under political indoctrination people collaborated for all sorts of reasons, such as taking the line of least resistance, fear, or greed, but only in a tiny minority of cases were the reasons ideological and, so far as this was concerned, the total results of the intensive Chinese program were, in the final analysis, no more effective than one might expect from an enthusiastic political rally. The Communists in many instances obtained collaboration from the American soldiers, but they produced few genuine converts. Brainwashing has its uses in extorting or manufacturing evidence for show trials, but it is doubtful whether as a method it is any more satisfactory in this respect than ordinary physical torture . . . For producing permanent converts it is useless" (Brown, 1963). *

Whereas the relative effectiveness of brainwashing is still open to some speculation, the persuasive value of "subliminal advertising" is not: it has none (Defleur & Petranoff, 1959; Goldiamond, 1959). Just what is subliminal advertising? It is a method whereby a communicator supposedly exposes you to a persuasive message without your being aware of it.

---

* Whether brainwashing will *ever* be an effective persuasive device remains to be seen. Based on the Chinese experience in North Korea, one is tempted to dismiss brainwashing as a persuasive device altogether. It should be pointed out, however, that the Chinese program was carried out under the most adverse circumstances for effecting ideological conversion. First, the American servicemen had the advantage of constantly reinforcing each other against becoming more receptive to the Chinese. Second, and perhaps as important as group resistance to conversion, Americans have not been trained to think in ideological philosophical perspective as have the Chinese. The Chinese were up against the problem of teaching American prisoners a way of thinking as well as what to think. Considering the difficulties faced by the Chinese, one can speculate that possibly, under more favorable conditions, brainwashing might be a more effective persuasive mechanism.

In the 1950's James Vicary announced that he had conducted an experiment demonstrating the power of subliminal advertising. He had arranged with a movie theater for the words "EAT POP-CORN" to be flashed on the screen periodically (during an on-going movie), just barely bright enough for the eye to pick up the phrase and supposedly not bright enough for the audience to realize they were confronting an advertising message. Vicary reported subsequently that the sales of popcorn at the theater had gone up dramatically as a result of the subliminal stimulation. Without reviewing the details, we ask you to accept our judgment that this particular experiment was poorly controlled although imaginatively contrived. Thus, we cannot place any degree of confidence in Vicary's findings. We can place even less confidence in the assumption underlying subliminal advertising that an awareness of what one is being exposed to gives the individual the opportunity to defend himself against the persuasion attempt and that somehow, if you can "get into the mind" through "by-passing" the person's conscious awareness, then the mind is unequipped to exercise any critical control over behavior. Considering this underlying assumption, one wonders how anyone could believe subliminal advertising would work!

Israel Goldiamond, reporting to the New Jersey Commission on Subliminal Projection, discounted the supposed manipulative value of such appeals in a humorous broadside: "Many years ago, when the X-ray was first announced, the legislature of one of our eastern states passed a bill forbidding the use of X-ray machines in public theatres on the grounds that they might be used by unscrupulous men to peer through women's clothes. One can imagine the hysteria involved in this misunderstanding of this advance in science. Today, a misunderstanding of science is leading to hysteria over subliminal perception. I find it difficult to be alarmed over subliminal perception. I would suggest that, compared to the X-ray, which has had a lasting impact, the impact of subliminal projection upon us may be as faint as the images it presents" (Goldiamond, 1959).

What has been scientifically determined concerning subliminal advertising—that it is not an effective persuasive technique—also is true in the case of three other science fiction favorites: truth serums, hypnosis and electrical stimulation of the brain.

In the case of the so-called "truth serums" (commonly sodium amytal or sodium pentothal) Lawrence Freedman made the following observations in a *Scientific American* article back in 1960: "Experimental and clinical findings indicate that only individuals who have conscious and unconscious reasons for doing so are inclined to confess and yield to interrogation under the influence of drugs. On the other hand, some people are able to withhold information and some, especially character neurotics, are able to lie. Others are so suggestible or so impelled by unconscious guilt that they will decribe, perhaps in response to suggestive questioning, behavior that never in fact occurred" (Freedman, 1960). As is obvious from Freedman's observations, the persuader who depends on "truth drugs" to control a person's behavior is relying on a very unreliable and resistable form of persuasion.

In the study of hypnosis no sizable amount of scientific evidence has even been accumulated to indicate that a person in a hypnotic trance can be made to do something he would not voluntarily do in a waking state. A common story relevant to this point concerns a hypnotist who had a female subject, under hypnosis, perform all types of behavior at his command. Yet, when he asked the girl to remove her blouse she snapped out of her trance and sent the startled hypnotist reeling with a resounding slap across the face! In a recent investigation of hypnotic interrogation (Field & Dworkin, 1967) the authors concluded that if their results could be generalized then ". . . they suggest that hypnotic interrogation has some effectiveness only with a minority of subjects who are quite easily hypnotized, and is undependable with average or poor hypnotic subjects." Dr. Brown puts it this way: ". . . the committing of socially reprehensible acts under hypnosis cannot be excluded as a possibility, but it is of far too rare and unreliable a nature to be counted on by those with evil intentions" (Brown, 1963).

Finally, the application of electrical stimulation to the human brain [*] has proven particularly ineffective in modifying man's behavior, let alone controlling his actions (Heath, 1963, 1964; Bishop, 1964). Such results have been somewhat disappointing in view of the fact that animals lower on the phylogenetic scale (e.g., rats) display rigid and vigorous stimulus bound behavior in the face of such stimulation. Perhaps, as brain stimulation research with man progresses (it is just beginning), ways of controlling human behavior through its use will be found. Until that time, however, we must conclude that it is useless as a persuasive device (in addition to being difficult to install!).

---

[*] A typical electrical stimulation procedure involves implanting an electrode into the human brain so that stimulation can be administered intracranially in a specified location.

Suggested Readings: Brainwashing, etc.

(1) Field, P., & Dworkin, S. Strategies of hypnotic interrogation. *Journal of Psychology,* 1967, *67,* 47-58.

(2) Freedman, L. "Truth" drugs. *Scientific American,* 1960, *202,* 145-154.

(3) Goldiamond, I. Statement on subliminal advertising. In: R. Ulrich, T. Stachnik & J. Mabry (eds.), *Control of human behavior.* Glenview, Ill.: Scott, Foresman & Co., 1966.

(4) Heath, R. Electrical self-stimulation of the brain in man. *American Journal of Psychiatry,* 1963, *120,* 571-577.

(5) Schein, E. The Chinese indoctrination program for prisoners of war. *Psychiatry,* 1956, *19,* 149-172.

Many scientists studying the persuasive process have devoted themselves to seeking and finding deterrents to behavior control.

Somehow it seems fitting to conclude a book on persuasion with a chapter devoted, in part, to this topic. We would not want the reader to complete the text firm in the belief that psychologists are totally absorbed in the business of human manipulation! Such is not the case. * Many scientists studying the persuasive process have devoted themselves to seeking and finding deterrents to behavior control. Such research advances both the cause of man and the science of persuasion.

One of the major figures in the study of resistance to persuasion is the well-known psychologist William McGuire. His work on "inoculation" as a defense against persuasion is a milestone in the research literature.

Specimen studies

1. One of the "principles of persuasion" from Chapter 5 states: "The people you may want most in your audience are often least likely to be there." This "selective exposure" hypothesis—that people tend to expose themselves only to persuasive appeals with which they already agree—has been repeatedly supported in a wide variety of experimental settings. In a now-classic study, William McGuire and Demetrios Papageorgis set out to consider the implications of selective exposure behavior on an individual's susceptibility to persuasion. They reasoned this way: the mechanism of selective exposure should be an effective system by which the individual can maintain his attitudes so long as he is not involuntarily exposed to counterarguments against his point of view. But what happens to the person who is forcibly faced with persuasive appeals opposed to his beliefs? McGuire and Papageorgis argue that in this case the individual will be highly susceptible to such appeals. Why? Because he is poorly prepared to resist counterarguments. "Living in an ideologically monolithic environment, the person tends to under-

---

* In fact, most of the studies described in this book were devised to test psychological theory, to help build theory, or to try out a method of conducting a study. Thus, the primary interest of the investigators was not to manipulate behavior but to extend our knowledge of how people learn and how our personalities function.

estimate the vulnerability of his beliefs and the likelihood of their being attacked. Hence, he will have had little motivation or practice in developing supporting arguments to bolster his belief or in preparing refutations for the unsuspected counterarguments." Drawing on a medical analogy, the investigators compare the person who has entertained only one point of view with the individual "brought up in so aseptic an environment that he has failed to develop resistance to infection and, hence, although appearing in very good health, proves quite vulnerable when suddenly exposed to a massive dose of infectious virus." Continuing in a medical framework, the authors consider two "immunization" procedures that might strengthen the individual's "resistance" to persuasive counterattacks opposing his viewpoint: (1) "Supportive therapy": an extra dose of information in agreement with the person's viewpoint; (2) "Inoculation": a weakened form of the persuasive counterargument designed to build up the listener's defenses to stronger forms of the same communication. Concluding their argument by medical analogy, McGuire and Papageorgis hypothesize that the inoculation procedure will be superior to the supportive therapy approach in making the individual more resistant to persuasion.*

To test their hypothesis McGuire and Papageorgis exposed 130 university undergraduates to four cultural truisms:**(1) "Everyone should get a chest X-ray each year in order to detect any possible tuberculosis symptoms at an early stage"; (2) "The effects of penicillin have been, almost without exception, of great benefit to mankind"; (3) "Most forms of mental illness are not contagious"; (4) "Everyone should brush his teeth after every meal if at all possible." Each subject participated in two experimental sessions. In the first testing period subjects received either supportive therapy (arguments in favor of the cultural truisms) or inoculation messages (counterarguments against the truism together with refutations of these counterarguments) on the various truisms. Afterwards subjects responded to a 15-item scale which measured how "true" or "false" they thought the various truisms really were. In the second experimental session subjects were exposed to strong counterarguments opposing the cultural truisms, after which they were readministered the 15-item scale from the first session. The experimenters wanted to know: Which form of immunization—supportive

---

* The investigators also tested other hypotheses which are not discussed here.
** A cultural truism is a statement that appears so obviously true it is seemingly beyond dispute. The four truisms selected for this study satisfied such a definition: in a pretest students almost unanimously ranked the truisms as being "definitely true."

therapy or inoculation—would be more effective in counteracting the impact of the counterarguments?

Findings: (1) The inoculation procedure (weak counterarguments) was more effective in producing resistance to the persuasive appeals. (2) The supportive therapy procedure (additional information bolstering the cultural truisms) was of no real resistance value at all. In summary, of the two immunization procedures, inoculation provided the only effective resistance to the highly persuasive counterappeals (McGuire & Papageorgis, 1961).

Discussion

The McGuire and Papageorgis work has generated a sizable amount of research work on the role of inoculation in increasing man's resistance to persuasion. A comprehensive review of the inoculation approach has been provided by McGuire (1964) and work in the area continues (Anderson, 1967; Manis, 1965). McGuire's efforts have also stimulated other investigators, using different approaches, to explore the resistance problem (e.g., Tannenbaum, Macaulay & Norris, 1966). Here, then, is an example of how one investigator is furthering our understanding of the processes involved in the resistance to persuasion.[*]

Suggested Readings: Resistance to Persuasion

(1) Freedman, J., & Steinbruner, J. Perceived choice and resistance to persuasion. *Journal of Abnormal and Social Psychology,* 1964, *68,* 678-681.

(2) McGuire, W. Inducing resistance to persuasion. *Advances in Experimental Social Psychology,* 1964, *1,* 191-229.

(3) McGuire, W., & Papageorgis, D. The relative efficacy of various types of prior belief-defense in producing immunity against persuasion. *Journal of Abnormal and Social Psychology,* 1961, *62,* 327-337.

(4) Tannenbaum, P., Macaulay, J., & Norris, E. Principle of congruity and reduction of persuasion. *Journal of Personality and Social Psychology,* 1966, *3,* 233-238.

---

[*] For other examples of work in the resistance area see Freedman & Steinbruner (1964) and Kiesler & Kiesler (1964).

The field of persuasion will continue to have an impact on society. How much impact depends, in part, on the ethics of the scientists studying behavior control and the sophistication of the individuals exposed to persuasive appeals.

The time is past when the researcher could dismiss the question of the effects of his efforts on society.* Regardless of his own motivations in selecting a given subject for study, he must be aware of and prepared to do something about the consequences of his discoveries.

Should research findings that could lead to more effective persuasion for whatever goal be closely held within the scientific community? What is the probability that within the lifespan of most of us—say 1984—enough will have been learned about the techniques of persuasion to subvert many of us without our awareness that anything is happening? On a different value plane, what is the likelihood that the right research findings in the wrong hands could result in many of us buying products we do not really want, taking our vacations at places we really are not interested in, and generally behaving as consumers in ways that persuaders want us to behave?

One comforting answer to these questions is that we have little to fear from the consequences of continued research on techniques of persuasion. The more widely the findings of such studies are disseminated, the less likely that they can be used to the advantage of any one group. (The one situation in which our fears might be justified would occur with the advent of a totalitarian government that controls all mass media. In that situation we would have much more to be concerned about than merely the application of opinion change studies.) In buttressing these points, we refer to some of the judgments of a respected observer of persuasion phenomena. In an article in the *Harvard Business Review,* Professor Raymond Bauer has said some important things. Here is the gist of his thoughts (Bauer, 1958).

"Our concern over being controlled is nothing new. Every advance in knowledge of the way that the human mind works

---

* No volume on persuasion would be complete without some speculation on this topic. It is not our intention to be exhaustive on this question; such detail requires a book in itself (which is being written: Andrews & Karlins, 1971).

has led people to worry about how this new knowledge might be used to their detriment.

Unquestionably social science research has developed increasingly effective *means* of persuasion, but practitioners in the field are not able to exercise *more* persuasion. Why? Because the same knowledge that increases the effectiveness of the persuader also increases the sophistication of his audience, sharpens their critical facilities, and fortifies their skepticism."

In effect, Bauer has said that persuaders must keep up with research in persuasion not to be more influential than they are now, but to keep from losing whatever effectiveness they may have at present, as their targets go right on gaining in sophistication and immunity. The net effect is that ". . . persuaders have been in a race to keep up with the developing resistance of the people to be persuaded."

"My guess is that over the years the American people have developed resistance to manipulation at about the same rate that our techniques of persuasion have become more sophisticated and effective. I mean, of course, that *if the audience had remained the same,* our new techniques would be more effective than our old ones. But the audience has not remained the same. The pace of the race has grown swifter, but it is difficult to say who has gained on whom" (Bauer, 1958).

Some scientists do not agree with Bauer's evaluation and what they have to say is not as comforting to individuals concerned with the impact of scientific persuasion on human behavior. These behavioral investigators argue that recent research advances have opened a gap between the persuader and his audience, leading to a dangerous imbalance between what scientific persuasion can accomplish and what the individual can resist. Professor James McConnell put it this way: "Look . . . we can control behavior. Now, who's going to decide what's to be done? If you don't get busy and tell me how I'm supposed to do it, I'll make up my own mind for you. And then it's too late."

Who is right? Is it those who say the man on the street is keeping pace with efforts to sway him or those who claim the forces of scientific persuasion have outdistanced his defenses? At this point, paradoxically enough, the people who are themselves practicing persuaders (e.g., advertising men, public relations executives, politicians) are most likely to reflect Bauer's point of view that you have to run hard to keep up with an increasingly sophisticated public. On the other hand, scientists or investigators in the field whose expertise is in theory, not the implementation of theory, probably think that persuasion devices are more powerful than they really are. As we pointed out in the introductory chapter of this book, it is reasonable to assume that as techniques of persuasion continue to evolve from art to science, their effectiveness in controlling behavior will be enhanced. *How effective* remains to be seen; yet, there is every reason to believe that persuasion techniques will become more effective when exercised on a scientific basis. Such has been the case when other areas of human concern have been subjected to scientific methodology. *

It should also be noted that in the years since Bauer's article was published, the tempo of scientific progress in persuasion-relevant areas has quickened. Particularly awesome research advances have been scored in the realms of behavioral genetics (e.g., Muller, 1965), psychotherapy (e.g., Goorney, 1968; Davison, 1968—practitioners of the new "reinforcement therapy") and mind function (e.g., Krech, 1969). Then, too, there is the impact of the computer with all of its implications for violating individual privacy and self-dignity (e.g., Karlins, 1969).

The implications of progress in persuasion have been discussed by many investigators (e.g., Rogers & Skinner, 1956). It is the authors' contention that if Professor Bauer's viewpoint is to retain any semblance of accuracy in the face of continued progress (remember, the science of persuasion is relatively young), then we will have to have a very alert and knowledgeable public. The race between scientific progress and man's capacity to cope with that progress is quickening; humankind must have the motivation and intelligence to keep pace with its own discoveries. Also, the man on the street will probably need some assistance from scientists who are concerned with furthering knowledge *and* humanity equally. There is a certain irony in persuasion research and the science of behavior control generally: as it develops the power to free man's mind from

---

* Of course, practicing persuaders such as politicians have neither the temperament nor the training to exercise persuasion on a scientific basis, even if we were far more advanced in this field than we are. Up to now the persuasion practitioners whom we know and have worked with (and we have worked with quite a variety of them) rely primarily on intuition, on their personal "feel" for a situation, and on the advice of like-minded associates. When you think about it, why *should* a PR man suddenly turn into a Ph.D. psychologist, or even think like one?

worry (e.g., therapy) it also gains the means to enslave his thoughts. Like the atom, the science of persuasion is "neutral"; man determines whether research findings will be used to liberate or subjugate the human spirit; to serve or destroy; to cure or infect. The science of persuasion can become one of man's most valued benefactors if the research investigator considers the behavioral *and* ethical ramifications of his work. As Leonard Krasner emphasizes in his essay "Behavior Control and Social Responsibility": ". . . Behavior control represents a relatively new, important, and very useful development in psychological research. It also may be horribly misused unless the psychologist is constantly alert to what is taking place in society and unless he is active in investigating and controlling the social uses of behavior control" (Krasner, 1964).

Suggested Readings: Persuasion and the Social Welfare

(1) Andrews, L., & Karlins, M. *Requiem for democracy?* New York: Holt, 1971 (in preparation).

(2) Bauer, R. Limits of persuasion. *Harvard Business Review,* 1958, *36,* 105-110.

(3) Davison, G. Elimination of a sadistic fantasy by a client-controlled counterconditioning technique. *Journal of Abnormal Psychology,* 1968, *73,* 84-90.

(4) Goorney, A. Treatment of a compulsive horse race gambler by aversion therapy. *British Journal of Psychiatry,* 1968, *114,* 329-333.

(5) Krasner, L. Behavior control and. social responsibility. *American Psychologist,* 1964, *17,* 199-204.

(6) Krech, D. Psychoneurobiochemeducation. *Phi Delta Kappan,* 1969, *50,* 370-376.

(7) Muller, H. Means and aims in human genetic betterment. In: T. Sonneborn (ed.), *The control of human heredity and evolution.* New York: Macmillan, 1965.

(8) Quarton, G. Deliberate efforts to control human behavior and modify personality. *Daedalus,* 1967, *96,* 837-853.

(9) Rogers, C., & Skinner, B. Some issues concerning the control of human behavior: A symposium. *Science,* 1956, *124,* 1057-1066.

8

SOCIAL SCIENCE METHODS

The studies reported here made use of methods acceptable to the social sciences. Such methods help the researcher to be as thorough, deliberate, and unprejudiced as possible in carrying out his work. In a way they are like blinders; they minimize distractions and irrelevancies, and they focus attention on the subject matter under investigation. Among the characteristics of scientific methods, there are two that are especially worth discussing: repeatability and controllability.

If a study can be repeated almost exactly as it was originally conducted, it means two things: (1) it has been conducted step-by-step, with each step in the process known and accounted for, and with nothing creeping in that was not intended to be there; (2) another investigator, working independently, can repeat the study and corroborate or refute earlier findings. The physical scientist can often meet a more exacting standard of repeatability than the social scientist, even though they have both been trained in the same general principles of scientific method. For example, the research chemist may have relatively little trouble verifying his results. He creates the setting for the experiment, notes each step in the process as he goes along, knows the order in which the ingredients are added, their relative strength and purity, and all the other elements of procedure. Contrast this situation with that of a research psychiatrist attempting to deduce some of the mysteries of mental illness from his experiments with patients. Whatever hypotheses he develops from one set of studies often cannot be verified by repeating the work on the same patients, because he may have changed them in some way. They are no longer the same people they were before the original investigation. The social scientist may then take another course of action. For example, he may use the same subjects again, if he thinks that, even though altered, they are the best humans available for his purposes; or he may try to find other subjects who have not been experimented with, and whose characteristics are as close a match as possible to his original subjects when he first started working with them.

In addition to permitting a repetition of the study, good method allows the investigator to exercise maximum control over what is going on. The more controllable the procedure, the less guessing is needed to interpret the results. Cause and effect are easier to trace when the number of possible causes is held to a minimum. In his ability to control what he is doing, the physical scientist again has the advantage over the social scientist. To get back to the chemist, he has an opportunity to exercise precise control over much of his procedure. He can measure exact amounts of materials. Electronic machinery may help him determine the nature of the impurities that are present in his substances, etc. By contrast, consider the situation of the political scientist whose task is to determine the effect of an international event or crisis on public opinion. For example, when American astronauts landed on the moon, what change was there in the prestige of America among peoples in other countries? The investigator finds himself in a situation over which he has only minimal control. He can find out something about the present frame of mind of the public, but has no objective way of comparing attitudes after the event with attitudes before the event (unless the event has been anticipated by research). He can ask people to remember what their opinions were before the critical event, but he knows he cannot rely on their memories as a satisfactory source of information.

The above illustrations of the differences inherent in investigations undertaken by physical and social scientists represent extreme cases. The social scientists can usually carry on studies that more closely approach the goals of scientific method. Nevertheless, it is probably important in reviewing these studies on persuasion, to realize that the ideals of scientific method are aspired to but rarely achieved in investigations of the social behavior of people.

All of the research on persuasion reviewed here was conducted by one of two methods employed by social scientists: experimental method, and survey or statistical method.

Experimental method

A key characteristic of this method is that the experimenter manipulates the condition he is studying and observes the effect of the change on the subjects. Many of the conclusions in this book are based on experimental evidence. Take, for instance, the question of whether it is better persuasion technique to draw a conclusion for your audience or present the evidence that suggests the kind of conclusion you want, and let the audience draw it themselves. In the experiment described on page 11, the investigator prepared a recording of a talk on devaluation of currency which led up to a statement of conclusions favoring devaluation. The talk was presented to two groups. One group heard it just as it was. Before the other group heard it, the conclusions were removed from the end of the talk. The opinions of both groups were ascertained by the same questionnaire after exposure to the broadcast to see if the opinions of one group changed more and/or in a different direction from the opinions of the other group. A vital aspect of the experiment was that the experimenter had control over how much and what parts of the persuasive communication were heard by each segment of the audience. Since the groups were chosen to be similar in other respects, any differences between them in direction and amount of opinon change could be attributed to the experimentally introduced differences in the broadcasts.

Similar characteristics are found in many of the experiments described in this report. For example:

(1) *Uniformity* of presentation except for the condition being tested. This is less of a problem when the communication is in print. If the message is to be spoken, it is often recorded beforehand.

(2) *Adequate size of experimental groups.* Large enough so that extraneous factors do not have too much effect. The more subjects you use, the less chance that the sleepless night that one of them had can influence the results.

(3) *Use of control groups.* There is usually one more group than the number of conditions being tested. In a conclusion-drawing experiment, for instance, you would want one group to be exposed to the argument with conclusions omitted, another group to hear the argument with conclusions included, and still a third group which was not exposed to any argument, but whose opinions were measured along with the others. This control group provides a baseline for correctly interpreting the data from the other two groups.

Suppose that the issue you were using in the experiment was a pro and con argument on outlawing the Communist party in the United States. Assume that during the time you were conducting the experiment a noisy congressional investigation was starting on the same topic. You would not know what effect the news reports of the investigation had on the opinions of your subjects unless you had used a control group. If there was a change in the opinions of the control group (who had not been exposed to *your* communication) then you would have to make allowances for this when interpreting the data from the experimental groups.

(4) *Before and after measurement of opinion change.* Usually by means of questionnaires administered to the subjects before and again after they have been exposed to the communication. When it is to the advantage of the experiment to do so, the questionnaires are often disguised. A few key opinion questions may be scattered through a much larger questionnaire. Sometimes these key questions are not repeated on the "after" questionnaire in order to conceal the true purpose of the instrument. Instead, alternate forms of the questions are used.

Survey method

The survey or statistical method is less controllable and less easily verifiable than the experimental method, but under certain conditions does meet acceptable standards for both of these characteristics. In an experiment, the investigator controls the subject's environment: he measures opinion, then introduces a new condition, then measures opinion again. The statistical method can often be used when the "new condition" is not controllable by the investigator. For example, one way to measure the popularity of a candidate before election time is to ask people whether they would vote for him. The popularity exists when you make the survey. It is not something the pollster wants to tinker with or *can* tinker with. You can measure changes in popularity from time to time, but these are caused by conditions over which you, the investigator, have no direct control.

Another way the statistical method might be used is in evaluating the effectiveness of advertising appeals on people of different ages at different economic and educational levels. You have to take people as they come, and obviously cannot make an old person young and then old again in order to test the effects of age, as an experimental approach would require.

A chief concern of the investigator who is using the survey method is the size and composition of the sample. The value of scientific sampling procedures is that the opinions of a relatively small number of people can be used to estimate the opinions of a

much larger group. If you wanted to know how *all* the people living in New York City feel about a decentralized school system, or
the adequacy of their police force, you could find out by asking
carefully developed questions of a properly selected group of perhaps 2000 New Yorkers. The mathematical basis of sampling is
such that your chances of accurate prediction increase greatly as
you increase the size of the sample, but only up to a point. For
example (and much depends on the kinds of questions you are asking), if you started with 300 properly selected people in the sample,
an additional 300 would add considerably to the accuracy of your
prediction. But if you had already surveyed 5000 people, adding
5000 more would not improve the accuracy of your data appre-
ciably. The art of sampling has been perfected to such a degree
that the Bureau of the Census actually uses samples of a few thousand people to check on the accuracy of the census itself.

Along with the problem of how many people to survey is the
problem of whom to survey. The value of the survey results depends to a large extent on whether the right people were reached.
In a pre-election poll, for example, you would want to survey only
eligible voters; if possible, a further refinement would be to try to
survey only people who are likely to go to the polls.

In the course of evaluating a mass of information gathered by
the survey method during World War II about life in the American
army, a reviewer discussed one of the general criticisms of surveys:
too often the findings are so obvious that many of them are common knowledge (Lazarsfeld, 1949). After pointing out that it is
hard to find a form of human behavior that has not been observed
somewhere, the reviewer lists a few statements which are typical of
wartime survey findings and guesses the reaction to them of many
critical readers. In his words:

" (1) Better educated men showed more psycho-neurotic symptoms than those with less education. (The mental instability of the
intellectual as compared to the more impassive psychology of the
man-in-the-street has often been commented on.)

" (2) Men from rural backgrounds were usually in better spirits
during their Army life than soldiers from city backgrounds. (After
all, they are more accustomed to hardships.)

" (3) Southern soldiers were more able to stand the climate in
the hot South Sea Islands than Northern soldiers. (Of course,
Southerners are more accustomed to hot weather.)

" (4) White privates were more eager to become non-coms than

Negroes. (The lack of ambition among Negroes is almost proverbial.)

"(5)   Southern Negroes preferred Southern to Northern white officers. (Isn't it well known that Southern whites have a more fatherly attitude toward their 'darkies'?)

"(6)   As long as the fighting continued, men were more eager to be returned to the States than they were after the German surrender. (You cannot blame people for not wanting to be killed.)"

". . . But why, since they are so obvious, is so much money and energy given to establish such findings? Would it not be wiser to take them for granted and proceed directly to a more sophisticated type of analysis? This might be so except for one interesting point about the list. *Every one of these statements is the direct opposite of what actually was found.* Poorly educated soldiers were more neurotic than those with high education; Southerners showed no greater ability than Northerners to adjust to a tropical climate; Negroes were more eager for promotion than whites; and so on."

These examples certainly do not demolish the criticisms of those opposed to the survey method. They do, however, lend support to the belief that each bit of research should be considered and criticized on its own merits.

Comparison of experimental and survey methods

It has been observed that experimental data and survey data often lead to two different conclusions. Typically, when attempted persuasion is evaluated by means of the survey method, such as is often done in studies of voting behavior, the finding is that the opinions of relatively few people are changed. On the other hand, when a persuasion attempt is evaluated by means of experimental method, relatively many of the participants are found to have changed. In considering this difference in outcome between the two methods, one investigator has noted several factors that help to explain the divergencies (Hovland, 1959).

A first critical factor is that in an experiment everyone in an experimental group is exposed to the persuasive message. By contrast, in a survey study, the people who have been exposed to the persuasive message have exposed themselves voluntarily. For example, Democrats are likely to predominate at a meeting at which Democratic candidates speak. Obviously the survey would show smaller changes than the experiment, since the survey encompasses many people who were on the persuader's side to begin with. The experiment exposes people of many more shades of opinion in regard to the message, and thus stands a better chance of revealing change.

The elapsed time between exposure to the message and measurement of opinion is another factor responsible for differences between experimental and survey data. In a typical experiment on opinion change, audience opinion is often measured within a few minutes after exposure to the communication. This is a time when the opinion changes may be at their greatest. On the other hand, when the interviews for a survey are conducted, they may take place several days after the television commercial, or the newspaper article, or whatever the stimulus was that is being evaluated.

Still a third consideration is the relationship of the audience to the measurement attempt. Experiments are often carried on in classrooms, where the student-subjects are in a familiar, friendly setting. They are likely to be generally receptive to any communication which is part of the experiment.* Compare this situation with that of an interviewer ringing a doorbell and asking permission to ask questions of a member of the household. Even with the reassurances of the interviewer, many respondents may feel uneasy about stating views which may be used to help the electioneering strategy of a candidate whom they loathe or to improve the effectiveness of a TV commercial for a product about which they care little.

The fact that surveys often attempt to reach a representative cross-section of the population, while experiments often are conducted with college students as subjects (because of their availability) may also contribute to differences in findings of the two methods.

Finally, it is possible that surveys often show little attitude change as a result of a persuasion attempt, while experiments reveal a much larger degree of success because of differences in the types of issues discussed in the communications. Experimenters often try to choose issues which are most likely to show change, while survey researchers frequently set out to measure attitudes which are deeply rooted in the culture.

---

* Recent studies show this problem to be quite serious. See, for example, Friedman (1967); Rosenthal (1966); and Rosenthal & Jacobson (1968).

9

A FEW DEFINITIONS

Social science

This term is misunderstood by many people. Part of the difficulty may lie in the broad, unspecific way in which social scientists themselves often refer to their field. An acceptable, although unspecific, definition might be that social science is a developing body of knowledge about the way that people behave, both as individuals and with other people. Any new piece of information about people, however, is not necessarily eligible for inclusion in social science literature. The information must have been gathered by research methods which approximate the criteria of scientific investigation. This point is elaborated on in the previous section on methodology.

Propagandist

A propagandist is a person who uses the mass media in an attempt to persuade people to his point of view. Even though the term propaganda has been linked with persuasion for a selfish purpose, no such negative emphasis is intended when the terms propaganda or propagandist are used here.

Mass media

Media usable for the impersonal transmission of messages to large audiences (Hovland, 1954).

Group and group norm

For our purposes a group consists of two or more people, linked together by circumstances or by choice, who share certain opinions and beliefs, and who expect each other to behave in certain ways which are appropriate to the group. It might be worthwhile to note what is, and what is not, included within this definition. The family, the people at work, the neighbors, the couple that come over to play bridge are included. So are the board of directors of a corporation and the Congress of the United States. All of these groups meet the two stipulations in the definition: shared opinions and behavior expectations. Among the shared opinions and beliefs (or group norms as they are often called) of the neighborhood group, for example, are: what kind of people they would like to see move in; whether it is all right for a man to wash his car in front of the house on Sunday morning; if it is neighborly to fence in your yard, etc. In addition to these norms are the behavioral expectations: who takes the kids for a Sunday afternoon pony ride or an ice cream cone, etc. Not included by our definition of group are such classifications as *New York Times* subscribers, owners of 1970 Plymouths, or everyone whose education ended with the eighth grade. Useful as these classifications are at times, they do not meet our specifications of both shared opinions and behavior expectations.

Opinion and attitude

Unlike some others who have used these terms, we are using them interchangeably in this book. There is no consensus among social scientists about these terms. * One writer makes this distinction: opinions require thought, attitudes do not. When existing attitudes do not cover a new situation, the response to the problem is an opinion. Thus attitudes cover wider ground than opinions. A common characteristic ascribed to attitudes is their emotional tone. Some people distinguish them this way: you can have an opinion and feel neutral about it, but attitudes are always accompanied by some positive or negative feeling.

Another source makes an interesting comparison between opinion and fact. Statements of opinion are generally regarded as more difficult to verify than statements of fact. Usually classed as opinions are statements making inferences about intentions, motives, reasons, or predictions as to what will happen in the future or what might have happened under certain circumstances. A related characteristic separating opinions from facts is the degree of generality of the statements. Facts are more specific, opinions less so (Hovland, Lumsdaine & Sheffield, 1949).

---

* Kiesler, Collins and Miller note a variety of definitions of attitude and its components (Kiesler, Collins & Miller, 1969).

Our definition is modeled after one researcher's definition of attitude. Opinions or attitudes are the inferred bases for observed consistencies in the social behavior of individuals (Hart, in Hartley & Hartley, 1952). The key words should be examined. The idea that opinions or attitudes are "inferred" is one that is generally held. The only way you know if someone has a given opinion or attitude is to deduce it from his behavior (which includes but does not end with whether he says he has it). The idea that opinions or attitudes underlie "consistencies" in behavior is another important point. To illustrate, take someone who has an extreme antagonism to big business. This person may identify all big business with monopoly, may regard management's goal as the exploitation of human labor, may think of any profit as unjustifiably large, and may prejudge as guilty any top executive accused of a crime. This anti-business attitude is responsible for consistency with respect to one kind of group. If you knew enough about this person's attitudes, you might accurately predict how he might react the next time a similar situation arose. The idea that opinions and attitudes *underlie* consistent reactions has important implications for us as individuals, and for any propagandist who wants to change attitudes. For each of us, it means that we can go through most days expending less effort to mentally manage our world. Each new situation need not be evaluated and responded to separately. If the morning paper tells of a Russian proposal to share atomic knowledge with all nations, many people will simply react: "More of their phony propaganda." If there is a discussion over lunch about the latest political crisis in France, one of the group is likely to inject with little forethought: "Those French never could agree among themselves." And so it goes.

Our attitudes help us to economize on thought. We react to many events and people as stereotypes instead of as unique experiences (Karlins, Coffman & Walters, 1969). This economy aspect of our opinions and attitudes gives the propagandist an advantage. The politician does not have to win us over on every issue that he represents in order for us to vote for him. If he can get us to agree with him on one or two issues, then our opinion toward him may become a favorable one. Once that has happened, and the mention of his name evokes a favorable response in us, then we may find ourselves inventing reasons for agreeing with his stand on issues with which we were formerly in disagreement. By influencing only one of our attitudes, the propagandist may be affecting our reactions to many things.

AFTERWORD

In reviewing the literature on persuasion that has appeared during the past ten years and comparing it with the preceding ten which were summarized in the first edition of this book, we became interested in differences and similarities in the way in which researchers have been going about their tasks.

These past ten years *have* been a time of synthesis. There have been fewer scattered studies, and more attempts to design investigations to test an emerging viewpoint. Consequently, in conception and imagination, the past decade has been a decade of growth.

Yet, it is our opinion that too often the imagination and energy of investigators have not been expressed in the experimental settings they devise. We are still studying the handy college student an overwhelming proportion of the time. Too frequently our experiments are conducted within the environs of a psychology department or within the confines of an academic classroom where associations with the intellect, grades and other aspects of the student-teacher relationship are paramount.

We think the time is past due for corroborating findings on sophomores with findings on other segments of the public. We have discussed persuasive appeals with you at some length; yet we know that a good part of what we present has emerged from a homogeneous and rather constrained setting.

We applaud the emerging perspectives that attitude change studies have increasingly provided. We wonder when more investigators will be willing to invest the time and effort necessary to carry out their work in less convenient, less agreeable, but possibly much more productive settings.

BIBLIOGRAPHY

Asterisk denotes reference was suggested reading selection and/or specimen study.

Abelson, R., & Miller, J. Negative persuasion via personal insult. *Journal of Experimental Social Psychology,* 1967, *3,* 321-333.

Adorno, T., Frenkel-Brunswik, E., Levinson, D., & Sanford, R. *The authoritarian personality.* New York: Harper, 1950.

*Alexander, C. Consensus and mutual attraction in natural cliques: A study of adolescent drinkers. *American Journal of Sociology,* 1964, *69,* 395-403.

Allen, V., & Crutchfield, R. Generalization of experimentally reinforced conformity. *Journal of Abnormal and Social Psychology,* 1963, *67,* 326-333.

Anderson, L. Belief defense produced by derogation of message source. *Journal of Experimental Social Psychology,* 1967, *3,* 349-360.

*Andrews, L., & Karlins, M. *Requiem for democracy?* New York: Holt, Rinehart & Winston, 1971 (in preparation).

*Aronson, E., & Golden, B. The effect of relevant and irrelevant aspects of communicator credibility on opinion change. *Journal of Personality,* 1962, *30,* 135-146.

Aronson, E., Turner, J., & Carlsmith, J. Communicator credibility and communication discrepancy as determinants of opinion change. *Journal of Abnormal and Social Psychology,* 1963, *67,* 31-36.

*Asch, S. Studies of independence and conformity: I. A minority of one against a unanimous majority. *Psychological Monographs,* 1956 (No. 416), *70,* #9.

*Bauer, R. Limits of persuasion. *Harvard Business Review,* 1958, *36,* 105-110.

Becker, S., Lerner, M., & Carroll, J. Conformity as a function of birth order and type of group pressure: A verification. *Journal of Personality and Social Psychology,* 1966, *3,* 242-244.

Bennett, E. Discussion, decision, commitment, and consensus in "group decision." *Human Relations,* 1955, *8,* 251-273.

Bergin, A. The effect of dissonant persuasive communications upon changes in self-referring attitudes. *Journal of Personality,* 1962, *30,* 423-438.

Berkowitz, L., & Cottingham, D. The interest value and relevance of fear-arousing communications. *Journal of Abnormal and Social Psychology,* 1960, *60,* 37-43.

Berscheid, E. Opinion change and communicator-communicatee similarity and dissimilarity. *Journal of Personality and Social Psychology,* 1966, *4,* 670-680.

Bishop, M. Attempted control of operant behavior in man with intracranial self-stimulation. In: R. Heath (ed.), *The role of pleasure in behavior.* New York: Hoeber, 1964.

Bitter, J. Attitude change by parents of trainable mentally retarded children as a result of group discussion. *Exceptional Children,* 1963, *30,* 173-177.

Bowers, J. Language intensity, social introversion, and attitude change. *Speech Monographs,* 1963, *30,* 345-352.

Brehm, J., & Cohen, A. *Explorations in cognitive dissonance.* New York: Wiley, 1962.

Brewer, R. Attitude change, interpersonal attraction, and communication in a dyadic situation. *Journal of Social Psychology,* 1968, *75,* 127-134.

Brock, T. Communicator-recipient similarity and decision change. *Journal of Personality and Social Psychology,* 1965, *1,* 650-654.

Brock, T., & Becker, L. Ineffectiveness of "overheard" counterpropaganda. *Journal of Personality and Social Psychology,* 1965, *2,* 654-660.

*Brown, J. A. *Techniques of persuasion.* Baltimore: Penguin, 1963.

*Brown, R. Models of attitude change. In: *New directions in psychology, I.* New York: Holt, 1962.

*Bryan, J., & Test, M. Models and helping: Naturalistic studies in aiding behavior. *Journal of Personality and Social Psychology,* 1967, *6,* 400-407.

*Calvin, A. Social reinforcement. *Journal of Social Psychology,* 1962, *56,* 15-19.

Carlson, E., & Abelson, H. *Factors affecting credibility in psychological warfare communications.* Washington: Human Resources Research Office, George Washington Univ., 1956.

Carment, D. Participation and opinion-change as a function of the sex of the members of two-person groups. *Acta Psychologica,* 1968, *28,* 84-91.

*Carment, D., Miles, C., & Cervin, V. Persuasiveness and persuasibility as related to intelligence and extraversion. *British Journal of Social and Clinical Psychology,* 1965, *4,* 1-7.

*Carmichael, C., & Cronkhite, G. Frustration and language intensity. *Speech Monographs,* 1965, *32,* 107-111.

Carrigan, W., & Julian, J. Sex and birth-order differences in conformity as a function of need affiliation arousal. *Journal of Personality and Social Psychology,* 1966, *3,* 479-483.

*Carron, T. Human relations training and attitude change: A vector analysis. *Personnel Psychology,* 1964, *17,* 403-424.

Cartwright, D. Achieving change in people: some applications of group dynamics theory. *Human Relations,* 1951, *4,* 381-392.

Cohen, A. *Attitude change and social influence.* New York: Basic Books, 1964.

Coleman, J., Katz, E., & Menzel, H. The diffusion of an innovation among physicians. *Sociometry*, 1957, *20*, 253-270.

*Cook, T., & Insko, C. Persistence of attitude change as a function of conclusion reexposure: A laboratory-field experiment. *Journal of Personality and Social Psychology*, 1968, *9*, 322-328.

Corrozi, J., & Rosnow, R. Consonant and dissonant communications as positive and negative reinforcements in opinion change. *Journal of Personality and Social Psychology*, 1968, *8*, 27-30.

*Cromwell, H. The relative effect on audience attitude of the first versus the second argumentative speech of a series. *Speech Monographs*, 1950, *17*, 105-122.

*Cromwell, H. The persistency of the effect of argumentative speeches. *Quarterly Journal of Speech*, 1955, *41*, 154-158.

*Cromwell, H., & Kunkel, R. An experimental study of the effect on the attitude of listeners of repeating the same oral propaganda. *Journal of Social Psychology*, 1952, *35*, 175-184.

Dabbs, J., & Janis, I. Why does eating while reading facilitate opinion change?—An experimental inquiry. *Journal of Experimental Social Psychology*, 1965, *1*, 133-144.

*Dabbs, J., & Leventhal, H. Effects of varying the recommendations in a fear-arousing communication. *Journal of Personality and Social Psychology*, 1966, *4*, 525-531.

*Davison, G. Elimination of a sadistic fantasy by a client-controlled counter-conditioning technique. *Journal of Abnormal Psychology*, 1968, *73*, 84-90.

DeFleur, M., & Petranoff, R. A televised test of subliminal persuasion. *Public Opinion Quarterly*, 1959, *23*, 168-180.

Deutsch, M., & Gerard, H. A study of the normative and informational social influences upon individual judgment. *Journal of Abnormal and Social Psychology*, 1955, *51*, 629-636.

*Diab, L. Studies in social attitudes: II. Selectivity in mass communication media as a function of attitude-medium discrepancy. *Journal of Social Psychology*, 1965, *67*, 297-302.

Dornbusch, S. The military academy as an assimilating institution. *Social Forces*, 1955, *33*, 316-321.

Duke, J. Critique of the Janis and Feshbach study. *Journal of Social Psychology*, 1967, *72*, 71-80.

Eagly, A., & Manis, M. Evaluation of message and communicator as a function of involvement. *Journal of Personality and Social Psychology*, 1966, *3*, 483-485.

*Ehrlich, D., Guttman, I., Schonbach, P., & Mills, J. Post-decision exposure to relevant information. *Journal of Abnormal and Social Psychology*, 1957, *54*, 98-102.

*Elms, A. Influence of fantasy ability on attitude change through role playing. *Journal of Personality and Social Psychology*, 1966, *4*, 36-43.

Eysenck, H. *Dynamics of anxiety and hysteria*. London: Routledge and Kegan Paul, 1957.

Festinger, L. *A theory of cognitive dissonance.* Stanford, California: Stanford Univ. Press, 1957.

Festinger, L. Cognitive dissonance. *Scientific American,* 1962, *207,* 93-102.

Festinger, L. *Conflict, decision, and dissonance.* Stanford, Calif.: Stanford University Press, 1964.

Festinger, L., & Carlsmith, J. Cognitive consequences of forced compliance. *Journal of Abnormal and Social Psychology,* 1959, *58,* 203-210.

*Festinger, L., & Maccoby, N. On resistance to persuasive communications. *Journal of Abnormal and Social Psychology,* 1964, *68,* 359-366.

Festinger, L., Schachter, S., & Back, K. *Social pressures in informal groups: a study of human factors in housing.* New York: Harper, 1950.

*Field, P., & Dworkin, S. Strategies of hypnotic interrogation. *Journal of Psychology,* 1967, *67,* 47-58.

Fine, B. Conclusion-drawing, communicator credibility and anxiety as factors in opinion change. *Journal of Abnormal and Social Psychology,* 1957, *54,* 369-374.

*Fishbein, M. (ed.). *Readings in attitude theory and measurement.* New York: Wiley, 1967.

*Freed, A., Chandler, P., Mouton, J., & Blake, R. Stimulus and background factors in sign violation. *Journal of Personality,* 1955, *23,* 499 (abstract).

Freedman, J. Involvement, discrepancy, and change. *Journal of Abnormal and Social Psychology,* 1964, *69,* 290-295.

*Freedman, J., & Steinbruner, J. Perceived choice and resistance to persuasion. *Journal of Abnormal and Social Psychology,* 1964, *68,* 678-681.

*Freedman, L. "Truth" drugs. *Scientific American,* 1960, *202,* 145-154.

*Freeman, F., Weeks, H., Ashley, H., & Wertheimer, W. News commentator effects: a study in knowledge and opinion change. *Public Opinion Quarterly,* 1955, *19,* 209-215.

Friedman, N. *The social nature of psychological research: The psychological experiment as a social interaction.* New York: Basic Books, 1967.

*Garber, R. Influence of cognitive and affective factors in learning and retaining attitudinal materials. *Journal of Abnormal and Social Psychology,* 1955, *51,* 384-389.

*Gerard, H. Conformity and commitment to the group. *Journal of Abnormal and Social Psychology,* 1964, *68,* 209-211.

Gerard, H., Wilhelmy, R., & Connolley, E. Conformity and group size. *Journal of Personality and Social Psychology,* 1968, *8,* 79-82.

*Goldiamond, I. Statement on subliminal advertising. In: R. Ulrich, T. Stachnik & J. Mabry (eds.), *Control of human behavior.* Glenview, Ill.: Scott, Foresman, 1966.

*Goorney, A. Treatment of a compulsive horse race gambler by aversion therapy. *British Journal of Psychiatry,* 1968, *114,* 329-333.

Greenberg, B. "Operation abolition" vs "operation correction." *Audiovisual Communication Review,* 1963, *11,* 40-46.

*Greenberg, B., & Miller, G. The effects of low-credible sources on message acceptance. *Speech Monographs,* 1966, *33,* 127-136.

*Gruner, C. An experimental study of satire as persuasion. *Speech Monographs,* 1965, *32,* 149-153.

Gruner, C. A further experimental study of satire as persuasion. *Speech Monographs,* 1966, *33,* 184-185.

Gruner, C. Effect of humor on speaker ethos and audience information gain. *Journal of Communication,* 1967, *17,* 228-233.

*Haaland, G., & Venkatesan, M. Resistance of persuasive communications: An examination of the distraction hypotheses. *Journal of Personality and Social Psychology,* 1968, *9,* 167-170.

Hartley, E., & Hartley, R. *Fundamentals of social psychology.* New York: Knopf, 1952.

*Hartmann, G. A field experiment on the comparative effectiveness of "emotional" and "rational" political leaflets in determining election results. *Journal of Abnormal and Social Psychology,* 1936, *31,* 99-114.

Harvey, O., Hunt, D., & Schroder, H. *Conceptual systems and personality organization.* New York: Wiley, 1961.

*Haskins, J. Factual recall as a measure of advertising effectiveness. *Journal of Advertising Research,* 1966, *6,* 2-8.

Hastorf, A., & Cantril, H. They saw a game: A case study. *Journal of Abnormal and Social Psychology,* 1954, *49,* 129-134.

Heath, R. Pleasure response of human subjects to direct stimulation of the brain: Physiologic and psychodynamic considerations. In R. Heath (ed.), *The role of pleasure in behavior.* New York: Hoeber, 1964.

*Heath, R. Electrical self-stimulation of the brain in man. *American Journal of Psychiatry,* 1963, *120,* 571-577.

Hereford, C. *Changing parental attitudes through group discussion.* Austin: Univ. of Texas Press, 1963.

Hewgill, M., & Miller, G. Source credibility and response to fear-arousing communications. *Speech Monographs,* 1965, *32,* 95-101.

*Hobart, E., & Hovland, C. The effect of "commitment" on opinion change following communication. *American Psychologist,* 1954, *9,* 394 (abstract).

*Homans, G. The western electric researches. In: Hoslett (ed.), *Human factors in management.* New York: Harper & Brothers, 1951.

Hovland, C. Changes in attitudes through communications. *Journal of Abnormal and Social Psychology,* 1951, *46,* 424-437.

Hovland, C. Effects of the mass media on communication. In: G. Lindzey (ed.), *Handbook of social psychology.* Vol. II. Cambridge: Addison-Wesley, 1954, pp. 1062-1103.

Hovland, C. Reconciling conflicting results derived from experimental and survey studies of attitude change. *American Psychologist,* 1959, *14,* 8-17.

Hovland, C., Campbell, E., & Brock, T. The effects of "commitment" on opinion change following communication. In Hovland et al., *The order of presentation in persuasion.* New Haven: Yale Univ. Press, 1957.

Hovland, C., Harvey, O., & Sherif, M. Assimilation and contrast effects in reactions to communication and attitude change. *Journal of Abnormal and Social Psychology,* 1957, *55,* 244-252.

Hovland, C., & Janis, I. (eds.), *Personality and persuasibility.* New Haven: Yale University Press, 1959.

*Hovland, C., Janis, I., & Kelley, H. *Communication and persuasion.* New Haven: Yale Univ. Press, 1953.

*Hovland, C., Lumsdaine, A., & Sheffield, F. *Experiments on mass communication.* Princeton: Princeton Univ. Press, 1949.

*Hovland, C., & Mandell, W. An experimental comparison of conclusion drawing by the communicator and by the audience. *Journal of Abnormal and Social Psychology,* 1952, *47,* 581-588.

*Hovland, C., & Pritzker, H. Extent of opinion change as a function of amount of change advocated. *Journal of Abnormal and Social Psychology,* 1957, *54,* 257-261.

*Hovland, C., & Weiss, W. The influence of source credibility on communication effectiveness. *Public Opinion Quarterly,* 1951, *15,* 635-650.

Husek, T. Persuasive impacts of early, late, or no mention of a negative source. *Journal of Personality and Social Psychology,* 1965, *2,* 125-128.

Insko, C. Primacy versus recency in persuasion as a function of the timing of arguments and measures. *Journal of Abnormal and Social Psychology,* 1964, *69,* 381-391.

*Insko, C. *Theories of attitude change.* New York: Appleton-Century-Crofts, 1967.

Insko, C., Arkoff, A., & Insko, V. Effects of high and low fear-arousing communications upon opinions toward smoking. *Journal of Experimental Social Psychology,* 1965, *1,* 256-266.

*Janis, I., & Feshbach, S. Effects of fear-arousing communications. *Journal of Abnormal and Social Psychology,* 1953, *48,* 78-92.

Janis, I., & Field, P. Sex differences and personality factors related to persuasibility. In: Janis et al (eds.), *Personality and persuasibility.* New Haven: Yale Univ. Press, 1958.

*Janis, I., Kaye, D., & Kirschner, P. Facilitating effects of "eating-while-reading" on responsiveness to persuasive communications. *Journal of Personality and Social Psychology,* 1965, *1,* 181-186.

Janis, I., & Mann, L. Effectiveness of emotional role-playing in modifying smoking habits and attitudes. *Journal of Experimental Research in Personality,* 1965, *1,* 84-90.

*Jarrett, R., & Sheriffs, A. Propaganda, debate, and impartial presentation as determiners of attitude change. *Journal of Abnormal and Social Psychology,* 1953, *48,* 33-41.

Jones, E., & Gerard, H. *Foundations of social psychology.* New York: Wiley, 1967.

Karlins, M. Conceptual complexity and remote-associative proficiency as creativity variables in a complex problem-solving task. *Journal of Personality and Social Psychology*, 1967, *6*, 264-278.

Karlins, M. *The last man is out.* New York: Prentice-Hall, 1969.

Karlins, M., Coffman, T., & Walters, G. On the fading of social stereotypes: studies in three generations of college students. *Journal of Personality and Social Psychology*, in press.

Karlins, M., & Lamm, H. Information search as a function of conceptual structure in a complex problem-solving task. *Journal of Personality and Social Psychology*, 1967, *5*, 456-459.

*Katz, D. The functional approach to the study of attitudes. *Public Opinion Quarterly*, 1960, *24*, 163-204.

Katz, D., McClintock, C., & Sarnoff, I. The measurement of ego-defense as related to attitude change. *Journal of Personality*, 1957, *25*, 465-474.

*Katz, D., Sarnoff, I., & McClintock, C. Ego-defense and attitude change. *Human Relations*, 1956, *9*, 27-45.

Katz, E., & Lazarsfeld, P. *Personal influence.* Glencoe: The Free Press, 1955.

*Kelley, H. Salience of membership and resistance to change of group-anchored attitudes. *Human Relations*, 1955, *8*, 275-289.

*Kelley, H., & Volkart, E. The resistance to change of group-anchored attitudes. *American Sociological Review*, 1952, *17*, 453-465.

Kelman, H., & Eagly, A. Attitude toward the communicator, perception of communication content, and attitude change. *Journal of Personality and Social Psychology*, 1965, *1*, 63-78.

*Kelman, H., & Hovland, C. "Reinstatement" of the communicator in delayed measurement of opinion change. *Journal of Abnormal and Social Psychology*, 1953, *48*, 327-335.

*Kiesler, C., Collins, B., & Miller, N. *Attitude change: A critical analysis of theoretical approaches.* New York: Wiley, 1969.

Kiesler, C., & Kiesler, S. Role of forewarning in persuasive communications. *Journal of Abnormal and Social Psychology*, 1964, *68*, 547-549.

Kimbrell, D., & Luckey, R. Attitude change resulting from open house guided tours in a state school for mental retardates. *American Journal of Mental Deficiency*, 1964, *69*, 21-22.

*Kimbrell, D., & Blake, R. Motivational factors in the violation of a prohibition. *Journal of Abnormal and Social Psychology*, 1958, *56*, 132-133.

King, B. Relationships between susceptibility to opinion change and child rearing practices. In Janis, et al. (eds.), *Personality and persuasibility.* New Haven: Yale Univ. Press, 1958.

*Klapper, J. T. *The Effects of Mass Communication.* New York: The Free Press, 1960.

*Koeske, G., & Crano, W. The effect of congruous and incongruous source-statement combinations upon the judged credibility of a communication. *Journal of Experimental Social Psychology*, 1968, *4*, 384-399.

*Koslin, B., Haarlow, R., Karlins, M., & Pargament, R. Predicting group status from members' cognitions. *Sociometry*, 1968, *31*, 64-75.

*Kotler, P. Behavioral models for analyzing buyers. *Journal of Marketing*, 1965, *29*, 37-45.

*Krasner, L. Behavior control and social responsibility. *American Psychologist*, 1964, *17*, 199-204.

*Kraus, S., El-Assal, E., & De Fleur, M. Fear-threat appeals in mass communication: An apparent contradiction. *Speech Monographs*, 1966, *33*, 23-29.

*Krech, D. Psychoneurobiochemeducation. *Phi Delta Kappan*, 1969, *50*, 370-376.

Krugman, H. E. The impact of television advertising: learning without involvement. *Public Opinion Quarterly*, 1965, *29*, 349-356.

*Lambert, W., Libman, E., & Poser, E. The effect of increased salience of a membership group on pain tolerance. *Journal of Personality*, 1960, *28*, 350-357.

Lana, R. Familiarity and the order of presentation of persuasive communications. *Journal of Abnormal and Social Psychology*, 1961, *62*, 573-577.

Lana, R. Interest, media, and order effects in persuasive communications. *Journal of Psychology*, 1963, *56*, 9-13.

Lana, R. Controversy of the topic and the order of presentation in persuasive communications. *Psychological Reports*, 1963, *12*, 163-170.

Lana, R. The influence of the pretest on order effects in persuasive communications. *Journal of Abnormal and Social Psychology*, 1964, *69*, 337-341.

*Lana, R. Three theoretical interpretations of order effects in persuasive communications. *Psychological Bulletin*, 1964, *61*, 314-320.

Lana, R., & Rosnow, R. Subject awareness and order effects in persuasive communications, *Psychological Reports*, 1963, *12*, 523-529.

Lawrence, D., & Festinger, L. *Deterrents and reinforcement.* Stanford, Calif.: Stanford University Press, 1962.

*Lawrence, L., & Smith, P. Group decision and employee participation. *Journal of Applied Psychology*, 1955, *39*, 334-337.

Lazarsfeld, P., Berelson, B., & Gaudet, H. *The people's choice.* New York: Duell, Sloan & Pierce, 1944.

*Lefkowitz, M., Blake, R., & Mouton, J. Status factors in pedestrian violation of traffic signals. *Journal of Abnormal and Social Psychology*, 1955, *51*, 704-706.

Lerner, D. (ed.), *Propaganda in war and crisis.* New York: Geo. W. Stewart, 1951.

*Leventhal, H. Fear: For your health. *Psychology Today*, 1967, *1*, 54-58.

Leventhal, H., Jones, S., & Trembly, G. Sex differences in attitude and behavior change under conditions of fear and specific instructions. *Journal of Experimental Social Psychology*, 1966, *2*, 387-399.

Leventhal, H., & Niles, P. Persistence of influence for varying durations of exposure to threat stimuli. *Psychological Reports*, 1965, *16*, 223-233.

Leventhal, H., & Singer, R. Affect arousal and positioning of recommendations in persuasive communications. *Journal of Personality and Social Psychology,* 1966, *4,* 137-146.

Leventhal, H., Singer, R., & Jones, S. Effects of fear and specificity of recommendations upon attitudes and behavior. *Journal of Personality and Social Psychology,* 1965, *2,* 20-29.

*Lewin, K. Studies in group decision. In Cartwright and Zander, *Group Dynamics.* Evanston: Row, Peterson, 1953.

Linton, H., & Graham, E. Personality correlates of persuasibility. In: Hovland & Janis (eds.), *Personality and persuasibility.* New Haven: Yale Univ. Press, 1959.

*Lumsdaine, A., & Janis, I. Resistance to "counter-propaganda" produced by a one-sided versus a two-sided "propaganda" presentation. *Public Opinion Quarterly,* 1953, *17,* 311-318.

*Lund, F. The psychology of belief. *Journal of Abnormal and Social Psychology,* 1925, *20,* 174-196. Cited in Hovland, Janis and Kelley, *Communication and persuasion.* New Haven: Yale Univ. Press, 1953.

Manis, M. Immunization, delay, and the interpretation of persuasive messages. *Journal of Personality and Social Psychology,* 1965, *1,* 541-550.

*Marrow, A., & French, J. Changing a stereotype in industry. *Journal of Social Issues,* 1945, *1,* 33-37.

McGinnies, E. Cross-cultural studies in persuasion. II. Primacy-recency effects with Japanese students. *Journal of Social Psychology,* 1966, *70,* 77-85.

*McGinnies, E. Studies in persuasion: III. Reactions of Japanese students to one-sided and two-sided communications. *The Journal of Social Psychology,* 1966, *70,* 87-93.

*McGinnies, E. Studies in persuasion: V. Perceptions of a speaker as related to communication content. *Journal of Social Psychology,* 1968, *75,* 21-33.

*McGinnies, E., & Rosenbaum, L. A test of the selective-exposure hypothesis in persuasion. *Journal of Social Psychology,* 1965, *61,* 237-240.

McGuckin, H. The persuasive force of similarity in cognitive style between advocate and audience. *Speech Monographs,* 1967, *34,* 145-151.

*McGuire, W. Inducing resistance to persuasion. *Advances in Experimental Social Psychology,* 1964, *1,* 191-229.

McGuire, W. Attitudes and opinions. In: *Annual Review of Psychology,* 1966, *17,* 475-514.

*McGuire, W. J. The nature of attitudes and attitude change. In: G. Lindzey & E. Aronson (eds.), *The handbook of social psychology* (2nd ed.), Vol. III. Boston: Addison-Wesley, 1969.

*McGuire, W., & Papageorgis, D. The relative efficacy of various types of prior belief-defense in producing immunity to persuasion. *Journal of Abnormal and Social Psychology,* 1961, *62,* 327-337.

Milgram, S. Behavioral study of obedience. *Journal of Abnormal and Social Psychology,* 1963, *67,* 371-378.

Milgram, S. Group pressure and action against a person. *Journal of Abnormal and Social Psychology,* 1964, *69,* 137-143.

Miller, C. *The process of persuasion.* New York: Crown, 1946.

Miller, N. Involvement and dogmatism as inhibitors of attitude change. *Journal of Experimental Social Psychology,* 1965, *1,* 121-132.

*Miller, N., & Campbell, D. Recency and primacy in persuasion as a function of the timing of speeches and measurements. *Journal of Abnormal and Social Psychology,* 1959, *59,* 1-9.

Mills, J. Avoidance of dissonant information. *Journal of Personality and Social Psychology,* 1965, *2,* 589-593.

*Mills, J., & Jellison, J. Effect on opinion change of similarity between the communicator and the audience he addressed. *Journal of Personality and Social Psychology,* 1968, *9,* 153-156.

Mitnick, L., & McGinnies, E. Influencing ethnocentrism in small discussion groups through a film communication. *Journal of Abnormal and Social Psychology,* 1958, *56,* 82-90.

*Muller, H. Means and aims in human genetic betterment. In: T. Sonneborn (ed.), *The control of human heredity and evolution.* New York: Macmillan, 1965.

*Nahemow, L., & Bennett, R. Conformity, persuasibility and counternormative persuasion. *Sociometry,* 1967, *30,* 14-25.

*Newcomb, T. Persistence and regression of changed attitudes: Longrange studies. *Journal of Social Issues,* 1963, *19,* 3-14.

Orwell, G. *Shooting an elephant.* New York: Harcourt, Brace & World, 1950.

Powell, F. The effect of anxiety-arousing messages when related to personal, familial, and impersonal referents. *Speech Monographs,* 1965, *32,* 102-106.

*Public opinion index for industry. *Building opposition to the excess profits tax.* Princeton: Opinion Research Corporation, Aug. 1952.

*Quarton, G. Deliberate efforts to control human behavior and modify personality. *Daedalus,* 1967, *96,* 837-853.

Quay, L., Bartlett, C., Wrightsman, S., & Catron, D. Attitude change in attendant employees. *Journal of Social Psychology,* 1961, *55,* 27-31.

Raven, B. Social influence on opinions and the communication of related content. *Journal of Abnormal and Social Psychology,* 1959, *58,* 119-128.

Reitan, H., & Shaw, M. Group membership, sex-composition of the group, and conformity behavior. *Journal of Social Psychology,* 1964, *64,* 45-51.

Riestra, M., & Johnson, C. Changes in attitudes of elementary school pupils toward foreign-speaking peoples resulting from the study of a foreign language. *Journal of Experimental Education,* 1964, *33,* 65-72.

Roethlisberger, F., & Dickson, W. *Management and the worker.* Cambridge: Harvard Univ. Press, 1939.

*Rogers, C., & Skinner, B. Some issues concerning the control of human behavior: A symposium. *Science,* 1956, *124,* 1057-1066.

*Rohrer, J., & Sherif, M. (eds.). *Social psychology at the crossroads.* New York: Harper, 1951.

Rosenbaum, M., & Levin, I. Impression formation as a function of source credibility and order of presentation of contradictory information. *Journal of Personality and Social Psychology*, 1968, *10*, 167-174.

Rosenblatt, P. Persuasion as a function of varying amounts of distraction. *Psychonomic Science*, 1966, *5*, 85-86.

Rosenthal, R. *Experimenter effects in behavioral research*. New York: Appleton-Century-Crofts, 1966.

Rosenthal, R., & Jacobson, L. Teacher expectations for the disadvantaged. *Scientific American*, 1968, *218*, 19-23.

*Rosnow, R. Whatever happened to the "Law of Primacy?" *Journal of Communication*, 1966, *16*, 10-31.

*Rosnow, R. One-sided versus two-sided communication under indirect awareness of persuasive intent. *Public Opinion Quarterly*, 1968, *32*, 95-101.

Rosnow, R., & Goldstein, J. Familarity, salience, and the order of presentation of communications. *Journal of Social Psychology*, 1967, *73*, 97-110.

Rosnow, R., Holz, R., & Levin, J. Differential effects of complementary and competing variables in primacy-recency. *Journal of Social Psychology*, 1966, *69*, 135-147.

*Rosnow, R., & Robinson, E. (eds.). *Experiments in persuasion*. New York: Academic Press, 1967.

Rosnow, R., & Russell, G. Spread of effect of reinforcement in persuasive communication. *Psychological Reports*, 1963, *12*, 731-735.

Rowe, P. Order effects in assessment decisions. *Journal of Applied Psychology*, 1967, *51*, 170-173.

Roy, D. Quota restriction and goldbricking in a machine shop. *American Journal of Sociology*, 1952, *57*, 427-442.

Rubin, I. Increased self-acceptance: A means of reducing prejudice. *Journal of Personality and Social Psychology*, 1967, *5*, 233-238.

Sargent, L., & Webb, T. The radical speaker on the University campus—a study in attitude change. *Journal of Communication*, 1966, *16*, 199-212.

Sarnoff, I., & Katz, D. The motivational bases of attitude change. *Journal of Abnormal and Social Psychology*, 1954, *49*, 115-124.

*Scheidel, T. Sex and persuasibility. *Speech Monographs*, 1963, *30*, 353-358.

*Schein, E. The Chinese indoctrination program for prisoners of war. *Psychiatry*, 1956, *19*, 149-172.

*Schroder, H., Driver, M., & Streufert, S. *Human information processing*. New York: Holt, 1967.

Schulman, G. Asch conformity studies: Conformity to the experimenter and/or to the group? *Sociometry*, 1967, *30*, 26-40.

Sears, D., & Freedman, J. Effects of expected familiarity with arguments upon opinion change and selective exposure. *Journal of Personality and Social Psychology*, 1965, *2*, 420-426.

*Sebald, H. Limitations of communication: Mechanisms of image maintenance in form of selective perception, selective memory and selective distortion. *Journal of Communication,* 1962, *12,* 142-149.

*Shaw, M. A serial position effect in social influence on group decisions. *Journal of Social Psychology,* 1961, *54,* 83-91.

*Sherif, M. Social factors in perception. In Swanson, Newcomb and Hartley (eds.) . *Readings in social psychology.* New York: Henry Holt, 1952.

Sherif, M., & Hovland, C. *Social judgment.* New Haven: Yale University Press, 1961.

Sherif, C., & Sherif, M., (eds.) . *Attitude, ego-involvement and change.* New York: Wiley, 1967.

Sherif, C., Sherif, M., & Nebergall, R. *Attitude and attitude change.* Philadelphia: W. B. Saunders, 1965.

Silverman, I., Ford, L., & Morganti, J. Inter-related effects of social desirability, sex, self-esteem, and complexity of argument on persuasibility. *Journal of Personality,* 1966, *34,* 555-568.

Simonson, N., & Lundy, R. The effectiveness of persuasive communication presented under conditions of irrelevant fear. *Journal of Communication,* 1966, *16,* 32-37.

Singer, R. The effects of fear-arousing communications on attitude change and behavior. Unpublished doctoral dissertation, University of Connecticut, 1965.

Skinner, B. F. *Walden two.* New York: Macmillan, 1948.

Smith, C. The effect of anxiety on the performance and attitudes of authoritarians in a small group situation. *Journal of Psychology,* 1965, *58,* 191-203.

Sponberg, H. A study of the relative effectiveness of climax and anticlimax order in an argumentive speech. *Speech Monographs,* 1946, *13,* 35-44. Cited in Hovland, Janis and Kelley, *Communication and persuasion.* New Haven: Yale Univ. Press, 1953.

*Steiner, I., & Johnson, H. Authoritarianism and conformity. *Sociometry,* 1963, *26,* 21-34.

Stricker, L., Messick, S., & Jackson, D. Suspicion of deception: Implications for conformity research. *Journal of Personality and Social Psychology,* 1967, *5,* 379-389.

*Suedfeld, P., & Vernon, J. Attitude manipulation in restricted environments: II. Conceptual structure and the internalization of propaganda received as a reward for compliance. *Journal of Personality and Social Psychology,* 1966, *3,* 586-589.

*Tannenbaum, P. Effect of serial position on recall of radio news stories. *Journalism Quarterly,* 1954, *31,* 319-323.

*Tannenbaum, P. Initial attitude toward source and concept as factors in attitude change through communication. *Public Opinion Quarterly,* 1956, *20,* 413-426.

*Tannenbaum, P., Macaulay, J., & Norris, E. Principle of congruity and reduction of persuasion. *Journal of Personality and Social Psychology,* 1966, *3,* 233-238.

*Thistlethwaite, D., de Haan, H., & Kamenetsky, J. The effects of "directive" and "non-directive" communication procedures on attitudes. *Journal of Abnormal and Social Psychology*, 1955, *51*, 107-113.

Thistlethwaite, D., & Kamenetsky, J. Attitude change through refutation and elaboration of audience counter-arguments. *Journal of Abnormal and Social Psychology*, 1955, *51*, 3-12.

Thomas, E., Webb, S., & Tweedie, J. Effects of familiarity with a controversial issue on acceptance of successive persuasive communications. *Journal of Abnormal and Social Psychology*, 1961, *63*, 656-659.

*Walster, E., Aronson, E., & Abrahams, D. On increasing the persuasiveness of a low prestige communicator. *Journal of Experimental Social Psychology*, 1966, *2*, 325-342.

*Watts, W. Relative persistence of opinion change induced by active compared to passive participation. *Journal of Personality and Social Psychology*, 1967, *5*, 4-15.

*Watts, W., & McGuire, W. Persistence of induced opinion change and retention of the inducing message contents. *Journal of Abnormal and Social Psychology*, 1964, *68*, 233-241.

*Wegrocki, H. The effect of prestige suggestibility on emotional attitudes. *Journal of Social Psychology*, 1934, *5*, 384-394. Cited by Hovland in G. Lindzey (ed.), *Handbook of social psychology*, Vol. II. Cambridge: Addison-Wesley, 1954.

*Weiss, W. A "sleeper" effect in opinion change. *Journal of Abnormal and Social Psychology*, 1953, *48*, 173-180.

*Weiss, W. Opinion congruence with a negative source of one issue as a factor influencing agreement on another issue. *Journal of Abnormal and Social Psychology*, 1957, *54*, 180-186.

*Weiss, W. Emotional arousal and attitude change. *Psychological Reports*, 1960, *6*, 267-280.

*Weiss, R. Consensus technique for the variation of source credibility. *Psychological Reports*, 1967, *20*, 1159-1162.

Weiss, W., & Lieberman, B. The effects of "emotional" language on the induction and change of opinions. *Journal of Social Psychology*, 1959, *50*, 129-141.

*Weiss, W., & Steenbock, S. The influence on communication effectiveness of explicitly urging action and policy consequences. *Journal of Experimental Social Psychology*, 1965, *1*, 396-406.

Whittaker, J. Attitude change and communication-attitude discrepancy. *Journal of Social Psychology*, 1965, *65*, 141-147.

*Whittaker, J. Sex differences and susceptibility to interpersonal persuasion. *Journal of Social Psychology*, 1965, *66*, 91-94.

*Whittaker, J., & Meade, R. Retention of opinion change as a function of differential source credibility: A cross-cultural study. *International Journal of Psychology*, 1968, *3*, 103-108.

Whyte, W. *Is anybody listening?* New York: Simon & Schuster, 1952.

Whyte, W. The outgoing life. *Fortune*, July, 1953.

Whyte, W. The web of word of mouth. *Fortune*, November, 1954.

*Whyte, W. *Money and motivation.* New York: Harper, 1955. Chapter 10.

*Wicklund, R., Cooper, J., & Linder, D. Effects of expected effort on attitude change prior to exposure. *Journal of Experimental Social Psychology,* 1967, *3,* 416-428.

*Wilson, W., & Miller, H. Repetition, order of presentation, timing of arguments and measures as determinants of opinion change. *Journal of Personality and Social Psychology,* 1968, *9,* 184-188.

*Wright, P. Attitude change under direct and indirect interpersonal influence. *Human Relations,* 1966, *19,* 199-211.

*Zagona, S., & Harter, M. Credibility of source and recipient's attitude: Factors in the perception and retention of information on smoking behavior. *Perceptual and Motor Skills,* 1966, *23,* 155-168.

Zajonc, R. Social facilitation. *Science,* 1965, *149,* 269-274.

Zimbardo, P. The effect of effort and improvisation on self-persuasion produced by role-playing. *Journal of Experimental Social Psychology,* 1965, *1,* 103-120.

Zimbardo, P. (ed.). *The cognitive control of motivation.* Glenview, Ill.: Scott, Foresman & Co., 1969.

*Zimbardo, P., & Ebbesen, E. *Influencing attitudes and changing behavior.* Boston: Addison-Wesley, 1969.

*Zimbardo, P., Ebbesen, E., & Fraser, S. Emotional persuasion: Arousal state as a distractor. Unpublished manuscript. Stanford University, 1968.

*Zimbardo, P., Weisenberg, M., Firestone, I., & Levy, B. Communicator effectiveness in producing public conformity and private attitude change. *Journal of Personality,* 1965, *33,* 233-255.

INDEX